# Travel to Liverpool, England

## The History, Tourism Information and Guide

Author
Aaron Ellis.

Copyright © 2019 Sonittec Publishing
All Rights Reserved

First Printed: 2019.



**Publisher**:
SONITTEC LTD
College House, 2nd
Floor
17 King Edwards
Road,
Ruislip
London
HA4 7AE.

# Table of Content

# Summary

## Traveling Values

There are plenty of things one can gain from exploring different places such as new friends, new experiences and new stories. When you start exploring new places, you get a better understanding of the people living there including their culture, history and background.

Studies show that travelling can improve your overall health and enhance your creativity. Therefore, you need to take time out from your daily tasks, office responsibilities, hectic schedule and everyday pressures at least once in a year. Plan a tour to a new city with an open schedule and let life present you with the numerous opportunities that are waiting for you.

✓ Improves Social and Communication Skills

✓ Ensures Peace of Mind

✓ Helps you Get Original and Creative Thoughts

✓ Broadens Your Horizons

✓ Enhances your Tolerance for Uncertainty

✓ Boosts Up your Confidence:

✓ Gets you Real-life Education

✓ Creates Memories for Lifetime

✓ Creates Memories for Lifetime

✓ Helps you Have Fun

✓ Aids you Get to Know Yourself

One of the main benefits of travelling, especially to areas where your native language is not widely used, is that you learn how to communicate with all manner of different people. It could be communicating to find the way to your next destination or asking for the nearest restaurant.

We all have stress and tension in our lives. Traveling forces us to temporarily disconnect from our normal routine and it helps us appreciate the people and things you have around. As per a famous saying "we never know what we have until we lose it."

It is believed that if someone gets out of their comfort zone, the mind gets more creative. To develop new neural connections that trigger original and creative thoughts, you must explore new places and break out of your daily lifestyles.

Travelling helps you connect with different people from different cultures, and this is fatal to prejudice, bigotry and narrow-mindedness. Meeting people from different cultures and societies will help you see issues and daily life from many different angles.

While travelling, you will find yourself stuck in situations where things don't always go as planned. Such situations will help you learn to cope with the uncertainties in life.

Being in a place where you do not know anyone will assist you to gain confidence and presence of mind. You will develop the ability to cope with obstacles, which will make you a confident person and help you grow as a person.

Meeting different people from vast cultures and societies provides an education that is impossible to get in a traditional school, college or a university. There is no substitute for the real thing.

If you travel with friends and family members, traveling helps you build stronger bonds and make memories. You can also save memories of a lifetime by creating photo albums or sharing photos in social media

No matter how young or old you are, no matter your profession, there is always a time when the child in you wants to have some fun. When you travel, you do not care what you do at all and you can just break free from the norm.

While traveling, you might find yourself stuck in situations you would not ordinary experience in your daily life. Such a situation can help you understand yourself and how you react to such circumstances and prepare you for future similar situations.

Although traveling offers many benefits, it also has some disadvantages if not planned carefully. If you are a patient and taking medication for a disease, do not forget to carry your medication. Keeping jet lag pills handy saves you from unnecessary discomfort.

Those susceptible to allergies should carry allergy medication. Plan your tour in advance, prepare a checklist to keep yourself healthy while traveling and pack important items before you travel.

Travelling is good for the health so decide a place now and pack your bags. Remember, you only live once, so start traveling to different places and get some life-altering experiences.

# Introduction

Liverpool is the capital city of the metropolitan borough of Merseyside in England, United Kingdom, sitting along the eastern side of the Mersey Estuary. It was founded in 1207 but was not granted city status until 1880. It is the fourth most populous British city with a population of 552,267 in the built-up areas.

Historically, Liverpool was a part of the county of Lancashire.

The city's expanded greatly from the 18th Century, largely brought about through its status as a major port. Trade from the West Indies, Ireland and mainland Europe, coupled with close links with the Atlantic slave trade, furthered its economic expansion. By the early

19th century, 40% of the world's trade passed through Liverpool's docks, contributing to its rise as a major city. Liverpool is also well known for its inventions and innovations, particularly in terms of infrastructure, transportation, general construction, and in the fields of public health and social reform. Railways, ferries and the skyscraper were all pioneered in the city, together with the first societies for animal and child protection, the first schools for the blind, for working-men, and for girls.

Inhabitants of Liverpool are referred to as Liverpudlians but are also colloquially known as "Scousers", in reference to the local dish known as "scouse", a form of stew, although the word is synonymous with the Liverpool accent and dialect. The port has contributed to its diverse population, which has been drawn from a wide range of peoples, cultures, and religions, particularly those from Ireland. The city is also home to the oldest Black African community in the country and the oldest Chinese community in Europe.

Labelled the World Capital City of Pop by Guinness World Records, artists of Liverpool origin have produced more number one singles than any other. The popularity of The Beatles, Billy Fury, Gerry and the Pacemakers, and the other groups from the Merseybeat era, and later bands such as Echo & the Bunnymen and Frankie Goes to Hollywood, contributes to Liverpool being a tourist destination. It was the European Capital of Culture in 2008.

Liverpool is noted for its rich architectural heritage and is home to many buildings regarded as amongst the greatest examples of their respective styles in the world. Several areas of the city centre were granted World Heritage Site status by UNESCO in 2004. Referred to as the Liverpool Maritime Mercantile City, the site comprises six separate locations in the city including the Pier Head, Albert Dock and William

Brown Street and includes many of the city's most famous landmarks.

Liverpool is also well known for its strong sporting identity. The city is home of two Premier League football clubs, Liverpool F.C. and Everton F.C. The world-famous Grand National also takes places annually at Aintree Racecourse on the outskirts of the city.

# History

Liverpool began as a tidal pool next to the River Mersey. It was probably called the lifer pol meaning muddy pool. There may have been a hamlet at Liverpool before the town was founded in the 13th century. It is not mentioned in the Domesday Book (1086) but it may have been too small to merit a mention of its own. King John founded the port of Liverpool in 1207. The English had recently conquered Ireland and John needed another port to send men and supplies across the Irish Sea. John started a weekly market by the pool. In those days there were very few shops so if you wanted to buy or sell goods you had to go to a market. Once a market was up and running at

Liverpool craftsmen and tradesmen would come to live in the area.

As well as a weekly market the king gave the citizens of Liverpool the right to hold an annual fair. In the Middle Ages, a fair was like a market but it was held only once a year for a period of a few days. A Liverpool fair would attract buyers and sellers from all over northwest England.

King John divided the land at Liverpool into plots called burgages on which people could build houses. He invited people to come and live in Liverpool. Then in 1229, the king granted the people of Liverpool another charter. This time he gave the merchants the right to form themselves into an organization called a guild to protect their interests. In many medieval towns, the Merchant's Guild also ran the town. In Liverpool, the members of the guild elected an official called the Reeve to run the town on a day-to-day basis. The first mention of a Mayor of Liverpool was in 1351.

However Medieval Liverpool would seem tiny to us. Even by the standards of the time, it was a small town. In the 14th century, Liverpool probably had a population of about 1,000. It was not more than 1200. Many of the people of Liverpool lived partly by farming. Others were fishermen. Some were craftsmen or tradesmen such as brewers, butchers, blacksmiths, and carpenters. Furthermore, a little stream ran into the pool and it powered a watermill that ground grain into flour for the townspeople's bread. There was also a windmill Southeast of the pool.

In the Middle Ages some wine from France was imported through Liverpool but its main trading partner was Ireland. Skins and hides were imported from Ireland. Iron and wool were exported from Liverpool. Despite its small size Liverpool sent 2 MPs to Parliament in 1295.

Curiously Liverpool did not have its own parish church, only a chapel. (A chapel was a kind of 'daughter' church dependent on a parish church nearby). The first chapel in Liverpool was the Chapel of St Mary. By the middle of the 14th century, there was also the chapel of Our Lady and St Nicholas. St Nicholas is the patron saint of sailors, which was obviously appropriate to a port like Liverpool. By 1235 there was a castle at Liverpool.

## Liverpool In The 16th Century And 17th Century

In the 16th century Ireland was still Liverpool's main trading partner. In 1540 a writer said: 'Irish merchants come much hither as to a good harbor'. He also said there was 'good merchandise at Liverpool and much Irish yarn, that Manchester men buy there'. Skins and hides were still imported from Ireland. Exports from Liverpool at that time included coal, woolen cloth, knives, and leather goods. There were still many fishermen in Liverpool.

The port of Liverpool also benefited when English troops were transported to Ireland to put down rebellions in the 16th and early 17th centuries. The troops spent money in the town. Liverpool was growing at this time but it still had a population of only 2,000 in 1600. The population of Liverpool probably reached 2,500 by the time of the civil war in 1642. Like all towns at that time Liverpool suffered from outbreaks of the plague. There were severe outbreaks in 1558 and 1609, 1647 and 1650. Meanwhile, in 1515, a grammar school was founded in Liverpool.

In 1642 the civil war between king and parliament began. At first, Liverpool was in the royalist's hands but in May 1643 Parliamentarian soldiers took the town. They dug ditches and erected earth ramparts around Liverpool to defend it from the royalist attack. In June 1644 Prince Rupert led a royalist army to try and re-capture Liverpool. He described the town as a 'mere crows nest which a parcel of boys could take'. At first, attacks were repulsed but then the Parliamentary troops left by sea leaving the people of Liverpool to defend their town themselves. The royalists attacked Liverpool one night. The townspeople resisted fiercely but were overcome. Many of them were killed. The royalist troops then sacked Liverpool. However, Liverpool only remained in the royalist's hands for a matter of weeks. In the summer of 1644, the royalists lost the battle of Marston Moor. Following the battle, they lost the whole of the North of England, including Liverpool.

Liverpool began to grow rapidly in the late 1600s with the growth of English colonies in North America and the West Indies. Liverpool was, obviously, well placed to trade with colonies across the Atlantic. The town boomed. In 1673 a New Town Hall was built on pillars. Underneath them was an exchange where merchants could buy and sell goods.

At the end of the 17th century a writer named Celia Fiennes visited Liverpool and gave it a glowing report. She said: 'Liverpool is built on the river Mersey. It is mostly newly built, of brick and stone after the London fashion. The original (town) was a few fishermen's houses. It has now grown into a large, fine town. It is but one parish with one church though there be 24 streets in it, there is indeed a little chapel and there are a great many dissenters in the town (Protestants who did not belong to the Church of England). It's a very rich trading town, the houses are of brick and stone, built high and even so that a street looks very handsome. The streets are well paved. There is an abundance of persons who are well dressed and fashionable. The streets are fair and long. Its London in miniature as much as I ever saw anything. There is a very pretty exchange. It stands on 8 pillars, over which is a very handsome Town Hall.' She also said: 'The town of Prescot stands on a high hill. It is a very pretty, neat town with a large market place and well paved, broad streets.'

In 1684 almshouses were built in Dale Street. They were followed in 1692 by almshouses in Shaws Brow. Then in 1699, Liverpool was finally made a parish of its own. The first parish church was St Peters, which was built in 1704. Meanwhile in 1660-78 parts of the castle were demolished. The rest was demolished early in the 18th century.

**Liverpool In The 18th Century**

In the early 1700s the writer Daniel Defoe also commented on Liverpool's booming trade. He said: 'Liverpool has an opulent, flourishing and increasing trade to Virginia and English colonies in America. They trade around the whole island (of Great Britain), send ships to Norway, to Hamburg, and to the Baltic as also to Holland and Flanders (roughly modern Belgium).'

In 1708 the Bluecoat School for 50 poor boys was built. (It was called that because of their school uniforms). The Royal Infirmary was founded in 1749. In 1754 a New Town Hall was built.

Georgian Liverpool grew rapidly. By the early 18th century it had probably reached a population of 5,000. By 1750 the population of Liverpool had reached 20,000 and by 1801 77,000. Many of the inhabitants were immigrants. In 1795 a writer spoke about 'the great influx of Irish and Welsh of whom the majority of the inhabitants at present consists'.

Many of the poor in Liverpool lived in dreadful conditions. Their houses were overcrowded and the streets were dirty. There were no sewers only cesspits. The worst houses were the cellar dwellings. The poorest people lived in cellars under buildings. Often they slept on piles of straw because they could not afford beds.

The first dock in Liverpool was built in 1715. Previously ships were simply tied up by the shore but as the port grew busier this was no longer adequate. Four more docks were built in the 18th century. Liverpool grew to be the third largest port in the country behind London and Bristol. It benefited from the growth of industries in Manchester. Since it was nearby port goods from Manchester were exported through Liverpool.

From about 1730 the merchants of Liverpool made huge profits from the slave trade. The trade formed a triangle. Goods from Manchester were given to the Africans in return for slaves. The slaves were transported across the Atlantic to the West Indies and sugar was brought back from there to Liverpool. At the end of the century, a famous actor visited Liverpool. When he was booed he told the audience that every brick of their town was 'cemented with the blood of an African'.

In the 18th century sugar refining became an important industry in Liverpool. Shipbuilding also became a flourishing industry. Rope making also prospered. (Rope was, obviously, needed in large amounts by ships). In Liverpool, there was also some manufacturing industry such as iron working, watchmaking, and pottery. Meanwhile in the 18th century rivers were deepened to make it easier for ships to sail on them. The Mersey and Irwell were deepened in 1720 and the Sankey Brook in 1755. From 1748 night watchmen patrolled the streets of Liverpool at night and in 1778 a dispensary was opened in John Street were the poor could obtain free medicines.

The American War of Independence began in 1776. At first, it disrupted trade from Liverpool. Obviously, it ended trade with the colonies themselves but it also meant American ships attacked English merchant shipping trading with the West Indies. They captured the ships and tool their cargoes. In 1778 France, Spain and Holland declared war on Britain. That meant ships from Liverpool could attack French, Spanish and Dutch ships and take their cargoes.

**Liverpool In The 19th Century**

In 1801 the population of Liverpool was about 77,000 and by 1821 the population had reached 118,000. In 1835 the boundaries of Liverpool were extended to include Kirkdale and parts of Toxteth and West Derby. By 1851 the population of Liverpool had reached 376,000. There were many Irish immigrants to

Liverpool in the early 19th century. Their numbers reached a peak during the potato famine in the 1840s.

At the end of the 18th century, sea bathing became fashionable among the upper and middle classes in England. They believed it was good for your health. In the early 19th century many people went sea bathing on the beach Northwest of Liverpool but in time newly built docks encroached on the beach. Meanwhile in 1802 Harthill Botanic Gardens were laid out.

The port of Liverpool boomed in the 1800s and many new docks were built. By the middle of the century, Liverpool was second only to London. The Manchester ship canal was completed in 1894. Although the docks dominated Liverpool there were other industries such as shipbuilding, iron foundries, glass manufacture, and soap making.

However Like all towns in the 19th century Liverpool was unsanitary. In 1832 there was a cholera epidemic in Liverpool. Another epidemic followed in 1849. Yet during the 19th century amenities in Liverpool improved. In 1799 and 1802 private companies began to supply piped water to Liverpool. But it was expensive and poor people could not afford it. They relied on barrels or wells. However, a municipal water supply was begun in Liverpool in 1857. The Philharmonic Hall was built in 1849. It burned in 1933 but it was rebuilt. The Central Library was built in 1852 and St George's Hall was built in 1854. William Brown library was built in 1860. Picton Reading Room was built in 1879.

In the 19th century amenities in Liverpool continued to improve. The Royal Southern Hospital opened in 1814. An eye hospital opened in 1820. The Northern Hospital followed in 1834. Stanley Hospital opened in 1867. The Walker Art Gallery opened in 1877. Stanley Park was laid out in 1870 and Sefton Park was opened in 1872. The Palm House was built in 1896.

Meanwhile from 1830 horse drawn buses ran in Liverpool and from 1865 horse drawn trams ran in the streets. The trams were converted to electricity in 1898-1901.

Liverpool officially became a city in 1880 and by 1881 its population had reached 611,00. In 1895 the boundaries of Liverpool were extended to include Wavertree, Walton, and parts of Toxteth and West Derby.

## Liverpool In The 20th Century

By 1901 the population of Liverpool had reached 685,000. In 1904 the boundaries of the city were extended again to include Fazakerley. In the early 20th century a number of notable buildings were built in Liverpool. The Tower Building was built in 1908. In the 1910s three of the most famous buildings in Liverpool were erected on the site of St George's dock, which had been filled in. The Liver Building was built in 1911. The Cunard Building was built in 1916. The Port of Liverpool building was also built at that time. The Lady Lever art gallery opened in 1922.

More than 13,000 Liverpudlians died in World War I. In 1921 a memorial was erected outside the Cunard building to all the Cunard employees who died in the war.

In 1928 a survey showed 14% of the population of Liverpool were living in poverty. This was, of course, much worse than what we would call poverty today. In those days poor people were living at bare survival level. In the early 20th century Liverpool suffered a shortage of houses. Overcrowding was common, as was slum housing. The council built some council houses but nothing like enough to solve the problem. Furthermore, Liverpool suffered severely in the depression of the 1930s and up to a third of men of working age were unemployed.

During the Second World War Liverpool was a target as it was, obviously, an important port. Some 3,875 people died in Merseyside and more than 10,000 houses were destroyed. Many more people were seriously injured and many more houses were damaged.

After World War II Liverpool council was faced with the task of replacing bombed houses. It also had to replace many slum houses. Like other cities, Liverpool 'redeveloped' central areas of the city in the 1950s and 1960s and many new council houses and flats were built. Overspill towns were built near the city at Kirkby and Skelmersdale Unfortunately demolishing terraced houses and replacing them with high rise flats broke up communities. In 1974 the boundaries of Liverpool were changed so it became part of an administrative area called Merseyside. Meanwhile, the Roman Catholic Cathedral in Liverpool was consecrated in 1967. The Anglican Cathedral was not completed until 1978.

In the later 20th century industries in Liverpool included engineering, cement manufacture, sugar refining and flour milling. For a time, in the 1950s and 1960s, the local economy boomed but it turned sour in the late 1970s and 1980s as Liverpool, as the rest of the country suffered from the recession. Liverpool became an unemployment black spot. One consequence of Liverpool's social problems were the Toxteth riots of 1981. In the last years of the 20th century, there were some hopeful signs. Liverpool remains a very important port. Because of its position in the Northwest, it is the main port for trading with North America. In the 1980s Albert Dock was redeveloped and turned into an area of bars, shops and restaurants.

From the 1980s Liverpool promoted tourism using its heritage as an attraction. Merseyside Maritime Museum opened in 1980. The Tate Gallery of Modern Art opened in 1988. The Museum of Liverpool Life opened in 1993. A Custom and Excise Museum opened in 1994. A Conservation Centre opened in Queens Square in 1996. Also in 1996 the Institute For Performing Arts opened.

**Liverpool In The 21st Century**

In the 21st Century Liverpool is still thriving. The National Wildflower Centre opened in 2001 and Liverpool was the European Capital of Culture in 2008. Then in 2012 Joe Anderson became the first elected mayor of Liverpool. In 2018 the population of Liverpool was 493,000

# People

As a port city active in maritime trade and experiencing considerable wealth prior to the 20th century, Liverpool has remarkable cultural diversity. Booming immigration from the Commonwealth, Ireland, and continental Europe all contributed to the diversity of nationalities and religions in the city. The years of prosperity are evident in the extravagant architecture of the buildings erected prior to the Great Depression, many of them places of worship for a wide variety of religions. Liverpool currently has a considerable Catholic population, but there are also Anglican, Greek Orthodox churches, mosques, synagogues and Hindu temples constructed throughout the city.

The population is predominantly white British, with considerably smaller populations of Asian British, Black British and mixed race individuals. Liverpool has the oldest community of Black British in all of England. Because of its shipping lines to Africa and the United States, freed slaves were some of the first Black settlers in the city. Liverpool also has the oldest community of Chinese in all of Europe, with the oldest Chinatown established by Chinese sailors in the 19th century. During the Great Irish Famine, the Irish population in Liverpool boomed and during periods of its history, Liverpool was notable for its considerable Welsh immigrant population. The cultural diversity of Liverpool has been contributed to by immigrants from the Caribbean, Latin America, Ghana and the Middle East.

There's a present community of LGBTQ individuals, and Liverpool has one of the only official gay districts in the United Kingdom. The Stanley Street Quarter is the site for the Liverpool Pride festival and has hotels, restaurants, nightclubs, cafes and shops.

Citizens of Liverpool are called Liverpudlians, but are more frequently referred to as *scouse* or *scousers*. The nickname is derived from the name of a stew that 19th-century sailors frequently made. Scouse can also refer to the accent of the |Merseyside District]], where Liverpool is located. The stew is still popular in the city and can be found on the menu at most pubs and restaurants.

Liverpool Football Club boasts an impressive number of trophies, more European trophies than any other English football club. The club's badge features the city's bird, the liver bird, inside a shield with twin flames on either side to commemorate fans who were crushed to their deaths against stadium fencing. Fans will sing the club's anthem, *You'll Never Walk Alone*, in chorus; a tradition begun in Liverpool that has now spread to other clubs across England and Europe. Just under a mile away are their bitter rivals Everton

Football Club. 'The Toffees', as they are nicknamed, features Prince Rupert's Tower in the club badge. Support for both clubs is strong and many families are divided on their loyalties.

Scousers boast their own distinct dialect, filled with slang sometimes deemed impenetrable by outsiders. Tourists may be referred to as a *wool* or *woolyback* which means a non-scouser. *Belter* is used as a positive exclamation, and *devoed* or *gutted* are used as negatives. If you're in a busy tourist area you can describe it as *chocka*, *chocka block* or *rammed* to fit in with the locals. And if you go out in the evening, ask for a *bevvie* or *a few scoops* to order a beer like a real scouser.

# Politics

A seaside town on the western coast of the United Kingdom, Liverpool's primary industry was historically maritime. Much of its early wealth and population growth came from the slaving and seal trades. Because of Liverpool's sustained wealth from the shipping trade, there were opportunities for the working class and immigrants who came from across the UK and Europe. The growing population contributed their diverse cultures to the profile of the city and is represented in the architecture of religious buildings throughout Liverpool.

During the 20th century, Commonwealth immigrants were a fast-growing segment of the population and Liverpool was steadfastly considered a working class city. During the Great Depression and following the decline of manufacturing in the 1970s, the city experienced significant rates of unemployment higher than the rest of the country. The 21st century has seen Liverpool focusing on regeneration and promotion of its long history for incubating cultural titans. Now, tourism is a significant industry for the city, capitalizing on The Beatles and the numerous galleries, museums and landmarks it has to offer.

In 2004, Liverpool became a UNESCO World Heritage site. The six sites across the city mark its significance in world trade in the 16th and 17th century and contributions to maritime trade technology. Now with the influx of redevelopment revenue as well as greater attention from national politicians to revitalize the city, some fear the World Heritage sites are in peril and openly oppose some of the new construction.

The city itself is governed by two levels of elected officials. The Liverpool City Council is composed of 90 councillors from 30 wards across the city. The most recent election in 2011 saw the Labour Party take control of the council. The remaining seats went mostly to Liberal Democrats, with a scant few going to the Liberal Party and the Green Party.

Public service in Liverpool is effectively divided between two mayors. One Mayor is directly elected and responsible for the day-to-day operations of running the city as well as working with the Liverpool City Council. There is also a ceremonial Lord Mayor, a civil mayor elected by the city council. The Lord Mayor is responsible for promoting the city and working with local charities and community groups. They are effectively the face of the city council in the city.

Liverpool of the 19th and 20th centuries was dominantly Tory. However, the election of Margaret Thatcher in 1979 and monetarist economic policies contributed to the rocketing unemployment rates at the end of the century that took a long time to recede. The late 20th century also saw public sector labor strikes that resonated strongly with the working class.

Now with a younger population in the metropolitan area, the city is considered a Labour Party stronghold.

# Liverpool Travel and Tourism

It might be most famous for The Beatles, and its two high-flying football clubs but scratch the surface and you'll swiftly realise that there's more to Liverpool than sport and music. Its thriving cultural scene, historic architecture and irrepressible lust for life make this city an unforgettable travel destination.

Once hampered by a down-at-heel reputation, there's no doubt that Liverpool's industrial past is now part of its considerable charm. Thanks to decades of careful urban regeneration and its 2,500-plus listed buildings (that's more than any city outside London), the waterfront and other thoughtfully revitalised districts are packed with museums, galleries, bars and restaurants, some of the best shopping in Britain, and a host of gleaming and interesting hotels.

Liverpool has been recognised not once but twice by UNESCO. Its musical heritage and ongoing musical influence recently gained it the status of UNESCO City of Music, one of only 19 in the world. The waterfront area has been a UNESCO World Heritage Site since 2004, reflecting the city's global significance as a commercial port when Britain's empire was as its peak.

Albert Dock is at the heart of the heritage waterfront, closely followed by Stanley Dock, the historic commercial districts and the bustling cultural quarter around William Brown Street. Throw in some shiny new constructions and the iconic principal waterfront buildings of the Pier Head the Cunard Building, the Port of Liverpool Building and the Royal Liver Building, together known as the Three Graces and you get one of the world's most recognisable city skylines.

Nowadays, culture plays just as big a part in drawing in the punters as footie and the Fab Four. Liverpool holds more national museums and galleries than any other UK city outside of the capital. Its remarkable portfolio includes the award-winning Museum of Liverpool, the International Slavery Museum, Tate Liverpool and The Beatles Story, while the UK's museum of popular music, the British Music Experience (BME), is the latest arrival on the city's flourishing cultural scene.

As with music, sport continues to exert a hold on Liverpool, whether in the crowds that cram into the stands to watch Liverpool or Everton play, or the throngs of colourfully-dressed race-goers that turn out each year for the Grand National.

# Sightseeing in Liverpool

## What to see. Complete travel guide

Liverpool is a city in the North West of England. The city is located in the mouth of the Mersey River. This is the second largest export port of Great Britain. The historical part of the port city, including its main attraction, Albert Dock, was added to the list of UNESCO World Heritage Sites in 2004. Liverpool is the neighbor of the cities of Huyton and Bootle. The other bank of the Mersey River is the location of Wales and Birkenhead. Liverpool is internationally well-known primarily because of its old football clubs - FC Everton and FC Liverpool. For many people the city is the birthplace of the legendary group "The Beatles", which started its performances here in the 60s of the previous century. In 2008, Liverpool, together with Stavanger, Norway, received the status of a cultural capital.

Residents of the city are officially called "liverpudlians", but the nickname "scousers" is much more well-known. Locals have got this nickname thanks to lobscouse a pottage invented by Norwegian sailors and the main food of the poor port folk. People here speak a special dialect called scouse. Liverpool is internationally famous not only because of its legendary river port and The Beatles, but also because of large national horse races (Grand National Steeplechase). This lively city is worth visiting not only to see its places of interest, but also to enjoy great shopping, attend various sports competitions and participate in the nightlife of the city.

**Albert Dock.**

Without a doubt, Albert Dock is the most important sight of Liverpool. The dock was opened more than 150 years ago by Prince Albert, and it remains the symbol of prosperity of the city which once was the port of the international importance. Today, the huge complex of buildings named Albert Dock is home to numerous shops, cafes, bars, restaurants and museums. Travellers are recommended to visit Tate Modern Art Gallery and the Merseyside Maritime Museum. Not far away from Albert Dock you will find Head Pier, which is home to famous Royal Liver Buildings and the legendary Liver bird - another symbol of Liverpool. This is the place where tourists are welcome to make a ferry ride and enjoy a beautiful view of the city.

## Merseyside Maritime Museum.

Merseyside Maritime Museum is dedicated to everything connected with shipping and port life. In this museum visitors will learn about the history of the largest ports in the world and about their meaning to people who lived at the time. Often the port became the beginning of a new life for many people. For some of them life improved after that step, and someone it became even heavier. The museum is located in Albert Dock. Entrance is free.

## Liverpool Stadium.

The stadium is a home arena of FC Liverpool. This is also one of the most famous stadiums in the world. Excursions to the stadium are organized daily once an hour. During these tours you and other 49 lucky visitors will be able to enter locker rooms, press halls and even walk along the football field. It is better to book an excursion in advance. As a rule, all tickets for the forthcoming week are already sold out. The museum of the stadium can be visited at any time, but buying a ticket for a match is, unfortunately, almost impossible.

Probably, FC Everton is not as well-known as FC Liverpool, but the atmosphere in the stadium during the games with either of the clubs is comparable. Therefore, if you like football, don't hesitate to visit a match with Everton. As a rule, one can still buy a ticket for such a match on the day of the event. In any case, the stadium that is known as Goodison Park is a fantastic sports facility. Plastic chairs stand here on wooden stairs just like many years ago, and visitors are permitted to watch the match in close proximity to the field, which is itself a unique opportunity.

**Anglican Cathedral.**

The Anglican Cathedral is the largest cathedral in Britain and the fifth largest in the world. Without a doubt, this is one of the most important sights of Liverpool. The cathedral is located a little away from the center of the city. The towers of the cathedral feature stunning views of the city. Moreover, the entrance is free.

## Matthew Street.

This is the street from which the career of the legendary Fab Four started. Today, everything on this street is connected with the name of The Beatles - John Lennon memorial, the old entrance to the club Cavern (the place where The Beatles had their first concert), a store devoted entirely to "The Beatles." Mathew Street is also home to The Grapes pub, in which the musicians spent time drinking beer between their performances (at that time beer was not sold at Cavern). Nowadays, Mathew Street is a popular holiday destination with plenty of bars, clubs and pubs.

## St. George's Hall.

St. Georges Hall is, probably, the most beautiful building of Liverpool, at least, regarding its interior decoration. It is located in Lime Street. St. George's Hall was built between 1838 and 1854. It consists of the court, ballroom and concert halls. The building was closed because of restoration works during many years, and only in April 2007 it opened its doors to the public. You can visit St. George's Hall for free.

Liverpool is one of the most convenient cities for shopping its shopping area is very small and is mostly closed for vehicles, leaving it all to pedestrians. Most of the shops are located along Church Street. If you are looking for something special, be sure to visit Bluecoat Chambers, which sells handmade works of art. Cavern Walks is the best place to find designer goods. If you're interested in retro items, antiques and handmade goods, Quiggins Centre will be your best choice.

# Top architectural sightseeing and landmarks of Liverpool

## Ideas on City Exploration Routes

Of course, in order to feel the magnificent atmosphere of Liverpool, one needs to visit this place, walk on charming streets of the historical center, visit local cafes, and enjoy the look of the local landmarks - Port of Liverpool Building, Liverpool Metropolitan Cathedral, St. Georges Hall, Wellingtons Column, Anfield and many others. In order to make your virtual tour to the city more interactive, we offer an unusual opportunity to fly over every notable landmark of Liverpool. Simply start the video, and use the full-screen mode. Each landmark comes with extra information, containing a collection of interesting facts and a photo gallery. Let's go!

## Port of Liverpool Building, Liverpool

<u>Facts</u>: » The Port consists of several buildings. They symbolized the commercial prosperity and global significance of the Port.

» Some of its parts are located on the shore. Three buildings are used for administrative purposes. They are close to the Ventilating Tower and the part of the wall panel of the house. » There are monuments, one of which reminds of the dead engineers from Titanic.

» In the southern part, there is the Albert Dock with port and storage rooms. It was the first time when wood had not been used for the construction. It was built only of bricks, concrete, and metal. Here, hydraulic crane was tested for lifting heavy materials.

» In the building of the Port, you can also visit the Tate Gallery, the Maritime Museum, and the exhibition dedicated to The Beatles.

» There is the Stanley Dock with working mooring points and port facilities. The rectangular building built of red bricks in 1848 looks really impressive.

» It will also attract with the Tobacco Storage. It is one of the biggest brick buildings in the world.

» The exterior of the official building Port of Liverpool Building is decorated with a lot of columns, curly windows, and statues.

**Liverpool Metropolitan Cathedral, Liverpool**

Facts: » The Metropolitan Cathedral of Christ the King belongs to the Roman Catholic Church.

» The issue of its construction had arisen in the 30s. It is related to the increased population of the city.

» The round foundation of the cathedral stretches in a

cone with a glass top. The cathedral accommodates 2 000 parishioners.

» There are prayer seats on marble pedestals. They surround the altar of white marble.

» The ceiling narrows to the top. There are colorful glass windows at the edges.

» The round building has a diameter of 59 m. Its total area is 10 000 m2.

» The dome of the cult construction is a truncated cone, resembles a crown and a pointed tower. It is made of glass.

» Decorative elements were made specifically for the Metropolitan Cathedral.

» The organ consists of 4 565 pipes.

» Upon the order of the royal family, the construction lasted 5 years, from 1962 to 1967. The Metropolitan Cathedral of Christ the King is a working parish church.

» This cathedral won the global competition for design projects.

## St. Georges Hall, Liverpool

Facts: » In 1836, the campaign on supporting the construction of the cultural institution was launched. This complex should consist of several sectors of art history orientation.

» The contest was won by the 25-year-old architect. The new building was opened in 1854.

» The entrance to the St. George's Hall is decorated with the sculpture of Benjamin Disraeli. Benjamin Disraeli was a writer and a political figure.

» Statues of famous people who contributed much to the cultural development of the country remind of the purpose of the building.

» The exhibition and concert center consists of halls and rooms with an inimitable design. Columns of red granite uphold the dome.

» There is a big organ (1855) in the north wing.

» These premises are allocated for different purposes depending on the circumstances.

» It was the first time when the universal heating and ventilation system was developed for such a huge building. Big three-meter boilers are serviced by dozens of workers.

» The St. George's Hall is also famous for the fact that writer Dickens read his works here. When Liverpool gained capital status in 2007, the drummer of the Beatles performed some songs on the roof.

## Wellingtons Column, Liverpool

Facts: » The granite memorial was constructed in honor of Arthur Wellesley, the Duke of Wellington, with the support of the citizens. The construction dates back to 1865.

» The monumental Wellington's Column looks like a pedestal and a corrugated column on it. The rectangular foundation with 169 steps is made of sandstone. The column itself is granite. There is an integrated bronze plate at the sides of the 132-meter obelisk. There are also bronze eagles in the corners. The plate in the southern part depicts the last battle of Waterloo. Other sides depict the last fights of the English soldier.

» The prolonged column narrows to the top. On the

platform, there is the sculpture of the legendary political figure. The copper statue was made of the trophy weapon left by the enemy after the battle.

» The sculpture of the leader points at the place where the legendary battle took place.

» The memorial Wellington's Column is aimed at reminding of the historical event taking place in one of the settlements of Waterloo. It was the battle between Napoleon's army and allied countries' troops.

## Anfield, Liverpool

Facts: » Anfield is a sports center in Liverpool. Football matches between English clubs are held here.

» Four stands accommodate over 54 thousand football fans. The highest capacity (61 905 spectators) was recorded in 1952.

» After the tragedy happened at one of the stadiums that resulted in the death of about a hundred fans, seats for spectators appeared at Anfield.

» You can enter the territory of the sports ground through two gates. They are named after Liverpool coaches.

» The full-fledged owner of the stadium is the Fenway Sports Group Company.

» Initially, the land belonged to the owner of the brewery. He provided his consent for holding sports competitions in the plot for a fee. Then, the football pitch was built here.

» The first match took place in 1884.

» The first stand had a red and white facade. Then, it was made of wood and corrugated iron. The Kemlyn Road stand became console, which means that it was covered with polymeric coating. Its construction cost £350 000.

» There is a closed dome above the stands.

» The total area of the pitch is 101x68 m.

» You can enter it only through the turnstile by the ID card.

**Radio City Tower, Liverpool**

Facts: » The Radio City Tower is a 10-meter device that receives radio waves. The 138-meter St. John's Beacon

Tower is not only a historical monument, but also an excellent way to view the city and all its surroundings.

» The Radio City has owned the building since 1969, which is proved by the inscription on one of the walls.

» Originally, the construction should serve as a ventilation trunk but it was not used for these purposes.

» Queen Elizabeth II visited the opening ceremony.

» Initially, the skyscraper was called the St. John's Beacon. There was a restaurant turning around its axes. Nowadays, it does not work.

» In 1999, The Radio City Tower was equipped with modern appliances and a receiving unit. The Radio and TV Tower serves as a broadcast center.

» The turning facade and the floor have remained unchangeable. Today, the turning glazed platform is an observation one. You can reach it by high-speed lift. There are business offices and conference rooms in it.

» The worker of the radio station can take you on a sightseeing tour. You can watch the studio working through the window.

» The renovation of the building in 1999 cost £5000000. The main material used during the renovation was concrete.

# Family Tips with Kids

Family trip to Liverpool with children. Ideas on where to go with your child

Liverpool is a peaceful and picturesque city that would be a perfect vacation destination for families with children of all ages. Knowsley Safari remains the most frequently visited landmarks in the city. That is the place where visitors can see wild animals that were brought to the park from different parts of the world. The beautiful safari park with spacious cages has become home for tigers, rhinoceroses, lions, and other African animals. There are many interesting attractions for kids that will make them super excited. In addition to numerous playgrounds, children are welcome at special makeup stands, where animators can put on face paint that resembles different animals.

Underwater Street Children's Discovery Centre is a no less interesting entertainment center. This is the place where children can not only have fun but also learn much interesting about the world, different professions and sciences. Boys will have an opportunity to become builders for some time, and creative children will be happy to participate in various artistic and handcrafting master classes. The center offers various educational programs for children of all ages, so parents with both toddlers and school age kids are recommended to visit it.

It is safe to call Spaceport the most unusual entertainment complex in Liverpool. As you can guess from its name, this center is all about space theme. There is an interactive museum, visitors of which will be able to learn a lot of interesting information about the outer space. Various quests and fascinating experiments make a visit to the museum very exciting. Moreover, children are allowed to touch, hold in hands or even try in action nearly all the items exhibited.

They can try to put on real astronaut's gloves, play various space simulators, and listen to interesting lectures about distant planets.

There are quite unusual entertainment centers in the city. They would be a perfect destination for travelers who are tired of classic excursions and walking. Travelers with older children can consider going to Having A Bubble Football center where they can play football while wearing big air-inflated costumes. That's a truly unforgettable entertainment! Once you're tired, head to a charming café with several delicious signature dishes.

Spring City Trampoline Park is also a wonderful destination for travelers with children of different age. This park features trampolines and bouncy castles to fit any taste. There are special areas with an increased security level for small children. Both children and their parents are welcome to jump and enjoy attractions of the park. There are also fields for various games and a cute café with a special menu for children.

If you've always been dreaming about mastering the basics of rock climbing, The Climbing Hangar is exactly what you need. This artificial climbing facility offers climbing walls of different complexity levels. There are suitable walls for both children and adults. Besides that, the center has several assault courses. It is worth noting that all the activities are done under the guidance of experienced coaches.

Travelers with preschool age children are recommended not to neglect Acorn Farm. This farm is a wonderful choice for travelers who crave for open-air activities. In the farm, visitors can get acquainted with friendly domestic animals, master the basics of taking care of them, and, of course, feed the animals. In Acorn Farm, visitors will find numerous goats, pigs, horses, and donkeys. There are also several open-air cages with more exotic animals like meerkats. Children enjoy touching and feeding cute animals, so there's no wonder why the farm is very popular with travelers with children.

# Cuisine and Reaustrant

Cuisine of Liverpool for gourmets. Places for dinner - best restaurants

In Liverpool fans of gastronomic tourism will have to face a huge choice of elegant restaurants, cozy pubs and cafes that are always happy to serve guests and have prepared most unique meals for them. The Pan American Club café is a popular place of rest among both locals and visitors of the city. Here you will always find peaceful and relaxing atmosphere. On daytime the cafe offers widest choice of international dishes, and at night this place is a magnificent destination for lovers of cocktails and beer. Tourists, who love simple and tasty food, are recommended to visit The Living Room restaurant. Spacious halls of the restaurant are perfect for family holidays. During the daytime the restaurant offers to its visitors widest choice of first courses and salads, at night visitors are welcome to taste flavored fish with spices and wine.

60 Hope Street restaurant is a perfect place to relax between interesting excursions. The restaurant's menu includes dishes that are usually served in a classic European bistro. The Office restaurant is located in the business district of the city. It will be liked by tourists who prefer European cuisine. The restaurant's hall is distinguished by its elegance. Employees from nearby offices remain the main visitors of this restaurant. Sometimes this place is visited by tourists, who come to this district in search of attractions. Fusion is a stylish restaurant that is very popular among both tourists and locals. Tuna with olives remains the specialty of the place. Meat lovers should not forget to try a juicy steak.

Baby Blue is one of luxury restaurants of Liverpool. It is located next to the lounge bar with the same name. This restaurant is the best place for private meetings. Fans of Asian cuisine will never get bored in Liverpool as here is located an excellent restaurant Bar Grill. Various meat dishes and grilled vegetables, flavorful sauces and spices you will simply not find a better oriental restaurant in this city. Among the sports bar of Liverpool we should definitely mention "Coubertin", which offers to its visitors a great selection of beers, exotic cocktails and original snacks. The opening of the restaurant named The Everyman Bistro took place over thirty years ago. The dishes here are served as a "buffet". The restaurant is very popular among fans of beer as here you will find more than twenty varieties of this drink.

Seafood is the basis and the main ingredient of the regional cuisine in Liverpool. Local chefs use different varieties of seafood to cook delicious food. The majority of traditional dishes are very simple to cook, and their recipes appeared centuries ago. Yet during the Middle Ages, local people started cooking various fish soups. Nowadays, numerous travelers head to local pubs to try these dishes that have become the classical national food. Tuna is particularly delicious in local cafes and pubs tuna with olives is a typical regional dish in Liverpool. In addition to popular fish dishes, local pubs offer fantastic beer by the region's breweries, as well as unusual snacks.

If you happen to visit one of the national cuisine restaurants early in the morning, you will be able to try the typical breakfast that locals like the most eggs with bacon. The dish is usually served with various sausages, stewed beans, and French fries. It remains one of the most popular varieties of street food in the city. Crispy potato slices are also not rare in restaurants specializing in the national cuisine. Fried potatoes are the most popular garnish to meat and fish dishes.

When it comes to meat dishes, it would be a mistake not to mention different variants of steaks and medallions. Different meat varieties are used to cook popular meat dishes in the region. As a rule, meat is mildly cooked at local restaurants, so travelers are encouraged to specify the degree of doneness in advance. Meat ragouts are also very widespread in Liverpool's cafes and restaurants. Locals are particularly fond of dishes cooked in pots. Some varieties of ragouts have an unusual serving inside a loaf of bread. More upscale restaurants usually offer game cooked in accordance with old recipes.

The city has a very picturesque district called China Town. As one can guess from the name, this district is rich in restaurants and cafes specializing in Asian cuisine. It is a great place for everyone who wants to try various interesting delicatessen. It is also the right destination for travelers who like seafood and unusual desserts in the Asian style. If you want to eat like a typical resident of Liverpool, simply visit any local pub. Pubs usually offer a rich choice of meat snacks, beer, and ale. Various types of roasted sausages and bacon are a great addition to delicious beer. Local pubs have very democratic prices and will not ruin your travel budget. Sweet tooths may want to attend charming cafes that offer popular national pastries together with fragrant English tea

# Tradition and Lifestyle

## Colors of Liverpool raditions, festivals, mentality and lifestyle

Liverpool is the city in the north-west of England, located at the mouth of the Mercy River. It also the second largest export port of Great Britain. Liverpool is famous for its outstanding football clubs - Liverpool and Everton; and music fans recognize this city as the birthplace of the glorious band - the Beatles. However, if you do not belong to any of these categories, there is still a lot to see and be surprised about! A city with a rich history and traditions, a bizarre interweaving of antiquity and modern achievements ... Liverpool's attractions can be admired for hours.

The local people are officially called the "Liverpudlians", but their most common nickname is the "Scousers". This nickname, the Liverpudlians received thanks to the lobscouse soup, the invention of Norwegian sailors and the main food of the poor port folk. Local residents speak a special English dialect - the scouse; they add the letter "L" to the end of the words. This vibrant city is worth visiting for several reasons: extraordinary sights, amazing opportunities for shopping, numerous sports events, and vibrant nightlife.

When in the restaurant, it's customary to leave a tip for the service provided. The amount of remuneration should be 10% of the total amount of the order. In addition, give the tips for the waiters, maids and taxi drivers. If you are coming here with American dollars, euros, yens or any other currency but not pounds - better exchange the currency at home because the amount of commission charged by Liverpool banks is very high. Currency exchange requires your passport.

Do not forget to take the umbrella when going out for a walk. The weather here is extremely changeable. Local people appreciate politeness and considerate approaches in communication. Residents can consider disrespecting a lack of gratitude for the rendered service. Consider that the city has very high fines for violating the speed limit - from € 75 to € 2,900. No less severe punishment for other violations of traffic rules.

You will always find the telephone booth on the streets of Liverpool. They work on a card or through coins. The minimum price of a telephone card is € 10. The hotel rooms have a city telephone connection; however, it is not always convenient to use it, because the tariffs are very high. Preferential calls from a landline phone can be made on a weekend or on weekdays from 22:00 to 6:00. Internet cafes are widely distributed, and many large shopping centers, cafes, and bars provide free access to Wi-Fi.

The largest British festival, entirely dedicated to the music of the Black Continent, is held annually in the center of Liverpool. Africa Oye is the summer open air festival traces its roots from the streets concerts, which were organized by the Liverpool enthusiasts and the carriers of African culture in 1992. The main purpose of this festival was the destruction of a negative public stereotype about Africa, as well as the demonstration for a wide audience of the wealth of modern African art. By 2002, the festival had reached a solid international level, and the most popular public park of Liverpool became its usual venue.

For one weekend, Africa Oye festival turns the idyllic space of Sefton Park into the ethno-village boiling with energy and colors, reproducing the best that the African continent can surprise Europeans with. The festival presents itself as a multicultural project, therefore, in addition to a huge variety of genres of African music, its program includes the ethno-rhythms of Latin America, the Caribbean, as well as such popular styles as reggae, calypso, salsa, and juice. Acquaintance with the, traditions of the "cradle of humanity" can begin with a visit to a large folk fair, on the trays of which there are vivid examples of African culinary, fashion, handicraft and souvenir products.

In late August, the annual week of the Beatles band will take place in the Liverpool. This is the most significant event for each and one fan of this glorious Liverpool quartet. Dozens of music bands from all over the world come here, to the birthplace of the legendary quartet to play their favorite repertoire. The main International Beatleweek venue is at the famous Cavern Liverpool club on Matthew Street, where the musicians regularly performed. Plus, here you will find numerous exhibitions, auctions of rare thematic things and excursions to memorable places of the group. On the streets you can meet many celebrities, sometimes the festival is visited even by Paul McCartney himself - as a rule, presents new compositions.

The followers of Hendrix and Morrison will gather in the cradle of British rock on a consciousness-expanding musical festival - Liverpool Psych Fest. Although the psychedelic revolution of the 60's has long been the property of history, its images, and cultural heritage continue to stir the minds of creative people in the "digital age". One of the largest British festivals, dedicated to music, visual art, film, and psychedelic literature, takes place at the end of September in

Liverpool. The main venues of this fest are two large underground clubs - Camp & Furnace and District. They are located in the industrial part of the city. A ticket for two festival days costs 60 pounds.

# Cultural Sights to Visit

Culture of Liverpool. Places to visit - old town, temples, theaters, museums and palaces
The famous musical group The Beatles has remained the main symbol of the city for many years. One of the museums of the city is dedicated to the world-famous musicians. During an excursion dedicated to «the Beatles Story» you will see numerous interesting collections, which are one way or another connected with the work of the group.

The museum also exhibits music records of the band, their scenic costumes, as well as rare photographs and musical instruments. Also, the visitors of the museum can watch a fascinating film about the work of musicians, which was filmed in 1967. Tourists interested in history and archeology will be glad to visit

World Museum, which also exhibits several large collections. Archaeological finds make up a significant part of the museum's collection. You will also find collections devoted to various sciences and ethnology. Near the museum you will find a planetarium. Every day here are organized various interesting lectures.

The biggest cathedral in the UK is located in Liverpool. Its construction took place in the first half of the 20th century. This prominent religious monument is also known as one of the main symbols of the city. Metropolitan Cathedral, which attracts tourists by its unusual architecture, is a no less remarkable place of interest. Walker gallery is an important object of various excursions. This is one of the largest and most famous art galleries of the country. The majority of the gallery's exhibitions represent works of local artists. Many paintings were made more than two hundred years ago. The paintings depict the most important events in the history of Liverpool, as well as its natural and architectural attractions.

Liverpool will be loved by fans of sport. Here, on the territory of "Enfield" stadium, are played the games of the famous football club that has fans in every city of the world. If you want to learn a lot about the history of the city, you should definitely visit Merseyside Maritime Museum. There are also some very unusual places among the city's museums. For example, Customs & Excise museum will tell its visitors about the history of smuggling. Fans of art are advised to attend the excursion to the Tate Art Gallery, where you can see collections of works of Poussin, Rubens and other famous painters.

From an architectural point of view, Liverpool Philharmonic is simply amazing from the very first minutes. Built in the Art Deco style, the building cannot go unnoticed. Among other places of interest that must be viewed and visited, it is worth mentioning The Isla Gladstone Conservatory. This unique building will amaze even those who are used to having nothing surprising them, and it is architecturally attractive, as well as an excellent example of the Victorian era. The building is closed to the general public, however, weddings are held here. Located on Water Street, India Buildings is another interesting facility for those who like to view interesting structures.

Walking along Albert Dock will be a great addition to getting acquainted with the city. It is a beautiful promenade, and strolling along it, you can find sailing and floating ships, as well as interesting buildings such as the art gallery Liverpool Pictures, Echo Arena, Tate Liverpool. Walking a little further, you can find another miracle of architectural idea, building of Port of Liverpool, included in the UNESCO World Heritage List. This, along with the "Liverpool 4", is one of the most recognizable symbols of the city. The building was erected in the early 20th century in the style of classicism.

In general, everything in the city seems to be connected with the Beatles, including the famous institution "Casbah Coffee Club", where the band (unknown at the time) introduced its songs to the general public for the first time, "The Jacaranda Club", where the four performed being famous, the home of John Lennon "Mendips", where the creative path of the great musicians began, as well as the Beatles monument mounted on Pier Head. Even the Liverpool airport is named after the performer of the eternal hit called "Imagine".

Liverpool is famous for its tunnels. A huge network called Williamson Tunnels connects the city, inspiring hundreds of tourists to get acquainted with the mysterious and enchanting place. This is a real story that needs to be learnt, and subsequently, the locals will not fail to tell it in all its details. Even children will find it pleasant to visit the sights in the city just for this reason you need to visit Speke Hall, which has a special soothing atmosphere. It is impossible not to mention the building considered unique for Liverpool, "Princes Road Synagogue". The shrine is amazing not only from the outside but the interior as well, which is even more inspiring, and epithets like "as awesome as in a palace" comes readily to mind.

# Attractions and Nightlife

City break in Liverpool. Active leisure ideas for Liverpool - attractions, recreation and nightlife

Liverpool is a great destination for fans of night clubs and discos. Thus, Korova club is considered one of the most prestigious night entertainments in the city. Every week here are organized performances of famous DJs, as well as concerts of indie performers. Fans of beer will not find a better place than Philharmonic pub. There they will find excellent beer and exotic snacks, and will be able to enjoy rich entertainment program. The pub's interior institution is made mostly in dark colors, so you can expect there solitary and even mysterious atmosphere. The soft leather armchairs, handcrafted solid wood furniture and attentive staff have made Philharmonic one of the most favorite places for both residents and tourists.

Fans of hard rock will like Cavern night club. Its opening was held in 1957. In this club, four years after its opening, took place the first performance of the legendary Liverpool Four. Currently the club is a regular venue for numerous festivals and cultural events dedicated to The Beatles.

Besides entertainments, you will find a huge number of shops and markets in the city. Clayton Square shopping complex is the location of pavilions with clothes and shoes, musical instruments, sports equipment and other goods. Clothing and perfumes of famous brands are offered to visitors in a shopping mall named Cavern Walks. If your aim is to buy food, Matta's store is the best choice for this. In addition to usual food, here are sold various delicacies.

There is a shop in Liverpool that is dedicated exclusively to the famous band The Beatles. In the Beatles shop you can buy not only all records of the band, but also funny memorable souvenirs. In each district of the city are opened interesting book shops, antique and souvenir shops - shoppers will never be bored here.

Entertainment in Liverpool can please each and one fan of a good holiday. While in Liverpool, it is worth to visit numerous museums, galleries and concert venues. This city is perfect for cultural rest, or having the vacation with family. In the city, you will find a lot of clubs and concert halls, where amateur musicians perform. If you love some active entertainment - Liverpool has what to offer as well. Visit the football stadium, the home arena for FC Liverpool. Here you will also find the museum and sights. Moreover, numerous parks and squares for outdoor recreation locate here.

You can combine pleasant with useful by going to an interesting place, under a no less interesting name, Another Place. This is a modern landscape installation, which consists of a hundred sculptures of cast iron representing human figures (in human growth and weighing 650 kilograms each) that partially or completely stand in the water. This miracle can be found on the beaches of Crosby, a 15-minute drive along the coast from Liverpool. This beach is a great place for walking! You can also visit the Safari Park Nowsli with your offsprings. Not everyone has the opportunity to travel to Africa, but if you are in Liverpool, you have a chance to "visit" this hot country, higher in a rather cool one. In this park, you can see savanna animals and tropical plants.

Another luxury place for walking is Beach Formby Point. At Formby Cape, you can enjoy nature and a beautiful view of the massive sand dunes. Here you can easily see sand lizards and toads, so, lovers of photos, do not forget your cameras - the photos here are just magnificent! This promontory is a little further from Crosby's beach, half an hour's drive from Liverpool. The surroundings of Liverpool are the perfect place for hiking, which also cannot be avoided without musical discoveries. On one of the high hills, among the picturesque landscapes is a unique monument -

"Singing Ring". A huge sculpture of metal and concrete, three meters high, resembles a tree with its outlines; the main mystery of the monument lies in another. It sings! The unusual structure of the monument, which includes many metal pipes, allows him to make wonderful sounds with the slightest blow of the wind.

# Shopping in Liverpool

## Authentic goods, best outlets, malls and boutiques

The famous Liverpool One shopping and leisure complex is located in the central part of the city. The complex includes a shopping mall with more than 170 shops. Here visitors will be able to find clothes and accessories for every style and budget. Besides apparel, there are many shops that sell cosmetics, perfumes, and colorful souvenirs. The biggest cinema in the city is also open in Liverpool One. Besides that, there are a mini-golf field and many other entertainments. The complex even has a hotel, so fans of shopping can stay in the immediate vicinity to one of the most popular shopping destinations in the city.

Perhaps, The Beatles shop remains one of the biggest landmarks of the city. Not only music addicts and fans of The Liverpool Four visit this shop but also curious tourists who want to bring interesting and authentic souvenirs from their vacation in Liverpool. The choice of souvenirs is, indeed, a giant one. In The Beatles shop, visitors can purchase old vinyl records, beautiful posters, tableware with images of the band, and many other exclusive items. Many travelers visit this popular shop as a museum. The shop looks spectacular and, what's more important, the prices are quite affordable.

Wayfarers Shopping Arcade is one of the best places to buy premium apparel, shoes, and perfumes. The two-storey shopping mall has more than 30 shops of different specialization. There are also several popular restaurants and cafes. Another advantage of the shopping arcade is that there are several creative designer shops there. For example, visitors will find shops that sell exclusive designer bags and stylish clothes by young couturiers. If you don't plan to shop, the arcade is still worth visiting as there are several gastronomic pavilions that sell national delicacies and sweets.

Fans of Liverpool Football Club will be glad to visit the official shop that is open in Liverpool One. The shop, which is also known as the biggest shop in Europe of its type, sells colorful goods and souvenirs for football fans. Besides classic fan scarves, t-shirts, and funny hats, the shop sells exclusive Liverpool FC merchandise. Moreover, one more interesting service is offered to visitors personalized souvenirs on demand. All guests of the shop can select a drawing or inscription they like, and the shop's masters will add it to a t-shirt, mug, or any other item.

St John's remains one of the biggest shopping centers in Liverpool. It's has become home for more than a hundred shops of famous brands. The shopping center is particularly famous the specialized sports shops that sell apparel and other goods at very affordable prices. When it comes to branded shops, consider visiting Argos this shop will be liked by fashionistas. Besides that, there are several quality cafes and restaurants at St John's.

If your aim is to find quality but inexpensive clothes and shoes, head to Metquarter. This shopping center offers branded goods at affordable prices. Discounts and sales never end at Metquarter. Many visit the shopping center to dine in its Italian café, Carluccio's, that offers fantastic desserts and the most popular Italian dishes.

Perhaps, Quiggins is the most unusual shopping center in Liverpool. Simply every shop there is a unique one. The boutiques at Quiggins sell antiquities, vintage clothes and jewelry, and handicrafts. If you still couldn't find what you need among the items for sale, experienced craftsmen are always ready to make an exclusive order. Many tourists visit this shopping center as an exhibition in order to make photos of old items and designer goods. As all items sold at Quiggins are exclusive, they are quite expensive.

# Unusual Weekend

How to spend top weekend in Liverpool ideas on extraordinary attractions and sites

The favorite city of fans of the Beatles has many places where visitors can see models of the yellow submarine, including the airport of Liverpool. Naturally, a big share of excursions is also, in some way or another, connected with the famous band. However, that fact doesn't make some landmarks less unique or interesting.

If you crave for some unusual pastime, it's high time to make an excursion in a landing vehicle The Yellow Duckmarine. The latter is something average between a usual tourist bus (without a doubt, a yellow colored one) and a boat. The unusual vehicles are usually docked near Albert Dock as that is the traditional starting point of an amazing bus excursion to the most attractive places of Liverpool. When returning to the dock, don't be scared when the bus starts slowly moving into the water. That's not the end of the excursion the yellow bus miraculously turns into a motor boat, and passengers enjoy a refreshing ride to the docks.

If you consider yourself a fan of the Liverpool Four, don't limit your excursion program to visits to popular museums and souvenir shops. There are many secret places in the city, the symbolic meaning and wondrous history of which are known only to most devoted fans of the band. Mathew Street, for example, is a "holy" place for music lovers as that is the location of old Cavern Club the first concert venue of the Beatles. The club keeps working, but the entrance to it is currently located on another side of the street. Having visited the legendary place, do not hurry to leave the picturesque street as there is one more symbolic place nearby. That is The Grapes, the famous pub that was frequently visited by the band after concerts.

If music related excursions seem to become boring, it's time to do something different and head to Waterfront Street to explore its signature landmarks. The Three Graces architectural complex is worth visiting. One of the turrets of the building has the symbol of the city the two Liver birds. They are a true talisman of the city. Many locals believe that if the birds leave the turrets, that would be the last day of Liverpool. Are you now scared about the destiny of the city? Then hurry up to Waterfront Street to prove yourself that the small birds are safely attached to the turrets.

Liverpool suburbs are an ideal place for walking. Naturally, such a walk will not be deprived of some music discoveries. One of the high hills in the picturesque area is the location of a very unusual monument - Singing Ringing Tree. Well, the result of hard work of modern abstractionists can be only nominally called a tree. The giant sculpture made of metal and concrete is three meters high and only slightly resembles a tree. However, the main secret of the monument is not in its look. It does sing! The unusual structure of the monument includes numerous metal tubes that make sound with even the slightest blow of wind. These sounds miraculously combine into harmonious melodies. Is it hard to believe in that? Then visit the monument and see yourself that the repertoire of the singing tree is unique and endless.

Liverpool is not only about yellow submarines and music fans who wander on the streets, hoping to find rare vinyl records. It's also about football fans wandering on the same streets. These fans have another "holy" place the domestic Liverpool Arena. Every day, visitors are welcome to attend an excursion in the stadium. You will have an opportunity to visit sportsmen's changing rooms, take a look at workout areas and even see press conferences with internationally famous coaches and sportsmen

## Accommodation

### Extraordinary hotels

# Best choice for your unusual city break in Liverpool

## Holiday Inn Express Liverpool-Albert Dock

From Liverpool center - 1.6 km

In Liverpool, one can easily find many creative and unusual hotels, such as Holiday Inn Express Liverpool-Albert Dock that is located not far from the Beatles Museum. This hotel is open in a classic looking building that dates back to the 19th century. Initially, the building was used as a warehouse. Guests of this unusual hotel can book spacious rooms with old brick walls and arched ceilings. All guest rooms have large windows. Some of the windows still have old treillages that, however, do not ruin the special harmony of this place.

## Hard Days Night Hotel

From Liverpool center - 0.9 km

In Liverpool, travelers can easily find thematic hotels that are targeted at the Beatles fans, and Hard Days Night Hotel is no exception. This hotel is open in the central part of the Cavern neighborhood. Literally, every detail of décor at the hotel reminds of the famous Liverpool Four. Portraits of musicians can be seen in both rooms and public spaces of the hotel. Moreover, all the artworks are exclusive. On weekends, Live Lounge attracts visitors with its live music and signature treats, but Four Bar is still considered the most stylish part of the hotel.

## Yellow Sub

From Liverpool center - 1.4 km

Hotels, open in docked boats, are another striking peculiarity of Liverpool. In Albert Dock, you will find the real yellow submarine - Yellow Sub Hotel. As it's not hard to guess from its name, the hotel is completely dedicated to the Beatles and their music. The design is also a wonderful example of traditions of the 60s of the previous century. Only 8 guests can stay at the hotel at the same time. The submarine has three posh bedrooms with the exclusive design. Yellow Sub also features a stylish lounge decorated with golden disks of the Beatles and exclusive photographs of the internationally famous musicians. The submarine has even a modern kitchen and a beautiful open terrace perfect for admiring the most prestigious part of Liverpool.

## The Joker Boat
From Liverpool center - 1.4 km

There is one more unique floating hotel near the submarine - The Joker Boat. The beautiful lilac colored boat has only three guest rooms. The designer team of the hotel was inspired by Joker, an antagonist from the Batman series. Travelers, who decide to spend several days on Joker's boat, will be pleased with the stylish design, light wooden décor, and overall bright and colorful look. There are two charming bars in the boat News and Circo.

## Hoax Liverpool
From Liverpool center - 0.7 km

The most prestigious hostel in Liverpool, Hoax Liverpool, is also worth a mention. Despite the fact that Hoax Liverpool has all signature features of a hostel, it is considered one of the most prestigious and popular accommodations in the city. A large choice of rooms is one of the main advantages of the hotel. Travelers can book individual rooms for single visitors or large guest rooms with two-level beds perfect for groups. The famous Hatch concert venue is located in the territory of the hotel, so guests of the hostel will never miss a gig.

**Titanic Boat**
From Liverpool center - 1.4 km

Fans of the romantic and tragic story of Titanic will be pleased and surprised to know that there is luxurious thematic Titanic Boat Hotel in the city. Without a doubt, it's the most romantic floating hotel in Liverpool. Many elements of the hotel's design are exact copies of the legendary Titanic. For example, the lounge area has the same floor as in the original ship. Beautiful furniture made of dark wood and crystal chandeliers can be seen absolutely everywhere. Bedrooms are decorated with colorful retro style wallpapers and various premium textiles. Titanic Boat can serve only eight guests at the same time. Each bedroom has a unique look and comes with thematic designer accessories.

# Stylish Design hotels

### Stylish weekend in Liverpool - collection of top unique boutique hotels

### Novotel Liverpool Centre
From Liverpool center - 0.9 km

If you want to stay at a designer hotel in Liverpool, take a look at Novotel Liverpool Centre. It is absolutely safe to call this hotel a paragon of modern style and elegance. All guestrooms are made with dominating white color, and décor features light sorts of wood. Bright pillows and designer furniture of dark cherry color only add charm to guest rooms. Thanks to large windows, there is always pleasant natural daylight inside during the daytime. The hotel's lounge bar, Elements, is distinguished by the bright design and features stylish furniture of unusual shapes and interesting artistic lighting.

## Hampton by Hilton Liverpool City Centre
From Liverpool center - 1.4 km

Hampton by Hilton Liverpool City Centre will not disappoint travelers who enjoy staying in stylish accommodation. The design of this hotel is inspired by traditions of the past, which were mixed with modern fashion trends. Guest rooms and public spaces feature beautiful soft furniture in retro style with premium upholstery made of best textile. The décor looks complete with modern wooden furniture and large floor vases with flowers. In guest rooms, travelers will also find beautiful paintings of city landscapes. Panoramic windows of the hotel offer magnificent views of the Tate Liverpool Museum located nearby.

## Hilton Liverpool
From Liverpool center - 11.3 km

Hilton Liverpool is open in one of the most stylish and eye-catching buildings of the city. The hotel has more than 200 comfortable guest rooms with panoramic floor-to-ceiling windows. The design of these rooms is made in different color combinations. It is worth noting that only natural materials were used in the decoration. Each guest room features a posh king-size bed, soft furniture in cherry or dark-green shades, cute low tables made of wood, and attractive table lamps. Bathrooms have marble décor, and glass partitions and transparent elements of the design create a polished and complete look.

## Indigo Liverpool

From Liverpool center - 1.1 km

Bright colors and creative designer solutions are the advantages of Indigo Liverpool. Colorful mosaic carpets on the floor, designer furniture of bold shades, big colorful paintings in modern style on the walls, and creative looking chandeliers in club style despite the abundance of colors and non-standard décor, the interior looks harmonious and attractive. The décor of the hotel's restaurant is also very attractive and is made in cheerful white-and-yellow colors. All national dishes seem to be even more delicious in such a charming setting.

## Malmaison Liverpool
From Liverpool center - 1.4 km

Fans of the glamorous style will be nothing but impressed by the décor of Malmaison Liverpool . Elegant furniture in retro style mixed with various modern elements of décor make up the basis of the design of public areas. In guest rooms, travelers will find beautiful dark wooden décor. Pink pillows made of velvet and sheer textiles add a touch of sophistication and luxury. One of the best British cuisine restaurants in Liverpool, Brasserie, is also open in Malmaison Liverpool. For many years, the restaurant has been hosting various interesting culinary shows.

## ibis Styles Liverpool Dale St
From Liverpool center - 0.8 km

ibis Styles Liverpool Dale St is open in a beautiful historical building. Behind the modest façade of the building, you will find an incredibly colorful and creative design inspired by the famous Liverpool Four. Guest rooms are mostly made in white and feature attractive wall paintings dedicated to the band. There are special photographic wallpapers in some rooms. Colorful carpeting with intricate patterns and stylish furniture are a perfect addition to the style. Fans of comfort will be pleased to find a spacious bathroom also made in shades of white.

## Luxury Accommodation

Top places to stay in Liverpool - most luxury and fashionable hotels

**Crowne Plaza Liverpool City Centre**
From Liverpool center - 1.4 km

Travelers, who prefer to stay at luxurious hotels only, are recommended to pay attention to Crowne Plaza Liverpool City Centre. This posh hotel offers comfortable guest rooms with modern design and panoramic view of the Royal Liver building. One of the most important elements of the hotel's infrastructure,

Harbour Leisure Wellness Center is a must-visit place. Guests of Crowne Plaza get access to the 18-meter indoor swimming pool, a romantic relaxation area with Jacuzzi and sauna. There is also an outstanding cosmetic salon in the wellness center.

### Radisson Blu Hotel, Liverpool
From Liverpool center - 1.3 km

The name Radisson Blu Hotel, Liverpool has long become a synonym of prestige and modern style. Besides comfortable guest rooms with panoramic views of the Mersey River, the hotel offers a range of useful services. Travelers will be pleased to find a state-of-art gym and large swimming pool. Foodies will be not disappointed with high-class restaurants. The Automobile Association of Great Britain awarded Filini restaurant that specializes in Italian cuisine. There is also the White bar and restaurant, in which visitors can try Spanish cuisine, order elite spirits and traditional tapas snacks.

### BridgeStreet at Liverpool ONE

From Liverpool center - 0.9 km

When it comes to describing apart hotels, BridgeStreet at Liverpool ONE should be mentioned first as that is one of the most prestigious hotels in its category. Its spacious guest rooms feature elegant furniture made of light wood, leather sofas and armchairs. There are beautiful paintings of local landmarks and city landscapes in all rooms. In bedrooms, visitors will find panoramic floor-to-ceiling windows, and bathrooms look very attractive thanks to white tiles and glass. BridgeStreet at Liverpool ONE is a great choice for independent travelers who are used to living in the atmosphere of complete comfort.

## Liverpool Marriott Hotel City Centre
From Liverpool center - 0.4 km

Posh and elegant Liverpool Marriott Hotel City Centre would fit requirements of even most discerning travelers. Guests will be glad to stay in bright and spacious rooms with modern electronics each room has an iPod dock station and a big plasma TV.

Bathrooms are also well-equipped and come with hydro-massage bathtubs. Among the variety of extra services provided by the hotel, it is worth noting a big indoor swimming pool and Urban Peace beauty salon that offers a wide range of beauty treatments.

### The Print Works Apartments
From Liverpool center - 1 km

Tourists, who make a group travel to Liverpool, might find exactly what they want at prestigious The Print Works Apartments. This apartment hotel has a creative design with all parts of the apartments made in different styles. The bedrooms are made in black-and-white shades and look classy, while beige remains the main color of living rooms. Despite color combinations, the apartments look very harmonious and home-like. Each apartment comes with a kitchen that features beautiful wooden décor and bright accessories.

### Parr Street Hotel
From Liverpool center - 0.9 km

The elite Parr Street Hotel is open in the same building with famous recording studios, art galleries, and offices. Despite such "neighbors", the hotel is a peaceful and calm place. All guest rooms have a perfect insulation. In order to make their stay more exciting, guests are recommended to visit the stylish Studio 2 Bar, where they can try signature cocktails and listen to their favorite music. Thanks to a wide choice of guest rooms made in different styles, every traveler will easily find a fitting room at Parr Street Hotel.

# Hotels with History

## Preserved history of Liverpool: long-standing and historical hotels

If you want to indulge yourself in the history of the city, consider booking a room at Childwall Abbey by Marston's Inns. The exact date of opening of this mini-hotel is not clearly known. Locals and current owners of Childwall Abbey say it's the oldest hotel in Liverpool. Anyway, the age of the hotel is no less than 300 years. The small hotel, which offers only 7 guest rooms for travelers, makes up a complex with the famous same-named restaurant.

The design of the hotel is reminiscent of an ancient pub. The restaurant is also an old and respectable place that has proved its right to be called one of the best dining destinations in the city. That's the place where visitors can try amazing steaks and national delicacies cooked in accordance with ancient recipes, real home-made pasta, and desserts. The outstanding décor of the hotel is worth a separate mention. In some guest rooms, you will find antique beds with canopies, while other guest rooms have the fireplace. Public areas are also decorated with old furniture and genuine artworks.

## Hope Street Hotel

From Liverpool center - 1 km

Hope Street Hotel is open in an eye-catching historical building not far from the heart of the city. Even after a thorough reconstruction, the building has kept many elements of the original style. Old brick walls, which can be seen in both guest rooms and public areas, add special charm to the hotel. The design of rooms is made in a minimalist style in order to underline the historic atmosphere of the building. Guests will also find a prestigious international cuisine restaurant, London Carriage Works, and a stylish bar that offers more than 50 sorts of branded wine to its guests.

## Heywood House

From Liverpool center - 1.1 km

Fans of history will enjoy their stay at the hotel with a symbolic name - Heywood House. It is open in the building of the oldest bank in Liverpool that was thoroughly restored and has kept its flawless look. Despite expectations, inside the historical hotel, visitors will not find a collection of antique furniture. All rooms are made in colorful modern style and are decorated with stylish wallpapers with a beautiful pattern, velvet textiles of different shades, and modern paintings with the most famous landmarks of Liverpool. Public spaces, in their turn, feature many elements of the original design. Beautiful arched passages, steep ladders with beaten banisters, ancient clocks, and mirrors in heavy wooden frames all these elements of décor remind of the culture of the past.

Travelers, who enjoy staying in apartments, also have a chance to stay in an inimitable historic atmosphere if they make a booking in Richmond Apart-Hotel. The building of the hotel is one of the most important architectural landmarks of Liverpool. All apartments are made in a unique style, and some still feature ancient brick walls. Massive crystal chandeliers complete the look of the hotel. Guests of Richmond Apart-Hotel are always welcome in the wellness center and spa salon.

## The Britannia Adelphi

From Liverpool center - 0.5 km

The Britannia Adelphi is a truly unique hotel, the opening of which took place in 1826. For more than 200 years, the hotel has kept its original atmosphere of solemnity and historical charm. Unique antique furniture in guest rooms, beautiful chandeliers in medieval style and elegant sculptures simply every detail in this hotel breathes history. Spindles Spa is one of the most welcome additions to the hotel's infrastructure. The spa has an indoor swimming pool and cosmetic rooms.

# Romantic Hotels

Liverpool for couples in love - best hotels for intimate escape, wedding or honeymoon

**Atlantic Tower by Thistle**

From Liverpool center - 1.3 km

Atlantic Tower by Thistle is one of the best hotels in Liverpool for couples who want to enjoy a romantic vacation. The hotel offers charming rooms with beautiful views of the Mersey River. All rooms are made in modern style and are decorated with elegant purple-colored soft furniture. Having enjoyed the serene atmosphere, head to Vista restaurant and bar where visitors can try the most popular European cuisine dishes and best wine. In the evening, the hotel's restaurant is also the best place to admire the waterfront.

## The Sir Thomas
From Liverpool center - 0.7 km

Boutique hotel The Sir Thomas is a totally charming place with an atmosphere that is perfect for lovebirds. The décor of its guestrooms is both simple and unique at the same time. Furniture made of precious sorts of wood and retro style table lamps add a special charm. Even the menu of the hotel's restaurant is full of romantics and includes numerous fruit and berry desserts, many of which are impossible to find anywhere else, as well as classic dishes of the British cuisine. Don't forget to visit the bar at The Sir Thomas in order to see and try wine brought from different parts of the world.

## 62 Castle St
From Liverpool center - 1 km

The refined atmosphere of 62 Castle St boutique hotel never ceases to conquer hearts of romantic travelers.

All guest rooms of the hotel are made in individual style and distinguished by a large size. Spacious rooms feature elegant designer furniture of unusual shapes. Some rooms have stylish looking leather sofas and armchairs, and in other rooms, guests will find retro style furniture. 62 Castle St is traditionally chosen by travelers to host important events, such as weddings. There is a beautiful banquet hall at the hotel that still has the original historical décor with elements made of stone and wood. Any celebration in such a setting promises to be an unforgettable one.

Posh Pads (Liverpool 1)Posh Pads (Liverpool 1) is one of the most popular apart-hotels in the city. The design of this hotel is reminiscent of a posh resort hotel in some Arabian country. Elegant sofas with velvet upholstery and numerous pillows of different shapes and sizes, giant wall-size colorful paintings, elements of décor made of premium materials such as rare sorts of wood and marble a stay in such a luxurious setting will be hard to forget. The romantic apart-hotel is open in the famous Casartelli building that was constructed in the end of the 18th century. The historical chic of the building has found its perfect reflection in the modern designer look of the hotel.

## Signature Living
From Liverpool center - 0.8 km

Young couples often prefer to stay at Signature Living. This hotel would fit adherents of different types of sport. The hotel is open in a beautiful historical building not far from the center of the city. It has only six rooms, each of which is unique. One of the guest rooms has antique frescos on the ceiling, and in another room, guests will find priceless old furniture in romantic style. Young and active couples, who are used to ending their day in stylish entertaining venues, will be in love with the exclusive night club. The hotel is located not far from the famous Metquarter shopping center, so it is also very popular with fans of shopping.

## The Racquet Club
From Liverpool center - 1.2 km

The Racquet Club is a great choice for couples of all ages. This hotel has everything needed for a comfortable and peaceful stay. Its décor strikes with the abundance of antiquities. The hotel also exhibits an interesting collection of paintings by local masters. Guest rooms are made in classic shades, with some rooms featuring floor-to-ceiling windows. Ziba restaurant is the best place for a romantic dinner. The restaurant serves classic English cuisine. Don't forget to visit the hotel's bar and enjoy its charming and private setting.

# More things To See and Do in Liverpool

Where to start? There's so much to do in Liverpool city region, the only problem might be deciding exactly what to do first.

Cultural capital, birthplace of The Beatles and UNESCO world heritage site, Liverpool has world-class attractions, a proud sporting historyand beautiful outdoor spaces - making it the perfect location for a UK city break.

We're rightly proud of our first-class tourist attractions. Find information on Liverpool's Leading Attractions, Beatles Liverpool, museumsand galleries, our two cathedrals and much more on this site.

Liverpool is officially the World Capital of Pop, with more Number One hits than any other city. And you can hear live music anywhere from a top arena to an intimate bar-room venue.

With more than our share of fabulous theatres and comedy nights, night-time Liverpool is vibrant and energetic.

Families will also have a great time in Liverpool with lots of attractions suitable for all ages. The museums, libraries and galleries all have regular family-friendly events and exhibitions on.

From Premiership football to the world's most famous steeplechase, the finest stretch of championship golf and the most successful Rugby League club of the modern era, Liverpool city region's sporting heritage is unrivalled

# Maritime & Heritage

Liverpool is a city built on it's Maritime Heritage and world trade influence. Liverpool's waterfront became a UNESCO World Heritage Site in 2004, centred around Liverpool as a Maritime Mercantile city and this reflects the city's significance as a commercial port at the time of Britain's greatest influence.

The World Heritage Site stretches along the waterfront from Albert Dock, through to the Pier Head and up to Stanley Dock, and then up through the historic commercial districts, the RopeWalks area to end at St George's Quarter.

In 1715 the first ever commercial wet dock opened in Liverpool, the Old Dock, originally known as Thomas Steer's Dock. The Albert Dock on Liverpool's waterfront was an architectural triumph that opened in 1846 and was the first structure in Britain to be built from cast iron, brick and stone. By the late 19th Century, 40% of the world's trade was passing through Liverpool's docks.

Two years after the Albert Dock opened it was modified to feature the world's first hydraulic cranes. It was a popular store for valuable cargoes like brandy, cotton, tea, silk, tobacco, ivory and sugar.

You can even stay amongst the beautiful maritime heritage at the Titanic Liverpool Hotel on the historic Stanley Dock complex inside a beautifully converted dock warehouse.

Delve deeper into the maritime history of Liverpool's docks from the commercial trade to its busy ferry terminal at the Merseyside Maritime Museum located amongst the largest collection of Grade I listed buildings in Britain, the Albert Dock. Or take a free tour of The Old Dock that has been carefully preserved beneath the Liverpool ONE complex.

## Liverpool Cathedrals

*"If you want a Cathedral, we've got one to spare..." so goes the old Liverpool folk song. Located either end of the aptly-named Hope Street, Liverpool Anglican Cathedral and Metropolitan Cathedral of Christ the King (Catholic) are vastly different in architecture but both majestic and beautiful.*

Halfway along Hope Street, outside Hope Street Hotel, two bronze statues represent the life and work of Bishop David Sheppard and Archbishop Derek Worlock. The two religious leaders, working together and with others, were a uniting force in the city during the less prosperous years of the 1970s and 1980s.

Liverpool Anglican Cathedral: is Britain's biggest Cathedral, and took 74 years to build from the foundation stone being laid in 1904. Sir John Betjeman called it 'one of the great buildings of the world.' The Cathedral has a full programme of events and hosts many conferences, large-scale gala dinners and functions. The Tower is open every day and boasts spectacular views across the city.

The Metropolitan Cathedral of Christ the King: was originally conceived as a huge structure in a similar style to the neo-gothic Anglican Cathedral. Of that design, only the Lutyens Crypt was built and due to the pressures of war and rising costs, the design was abandoned. The current modern, circular Cathedral opened in 1967, and features modern works of art and glorious multi-coloured windows. The majestic barrel vaults of fine brickwork and granite pillars of the original Lutyens Crypt can still be seen.

## Metropolitan Cathedral Of Christ The King

Cathedral House, Mount Pleasant, Liverpool,

Merseyside, L3 5TQ

Tel: +44 (0)151 709 9222

No trip to Liverpool is complete without a visit to the awe-inspiring Metropolitan Cathedral of Christ the King. This dramatic icon of faith, architecture and human endeavour is spectacular in both scale and design.

Explore the Cathedral's majestic interior which includes modern works of art and stunning design features, such as its striking Lantern Tower - the world's largest area of coloured glass. Along with daily Masses and Services, the Cathedral runs a diverse programme of wonderful music concerts, exhibitions and special events..

Of special note is the magnificent Lutyens Crypt and Treasury, situated within the Cathedral. An architectural gem in its own right, the Crypt is one of the most significant works in this country of the leading British architect Sir Edwin Lutyens. Part of Lutyens' early 20th century Cathedral design, the Crypt offers a fascinating glimpse of what might have been, had it been completed. Don't miss a chance to explore this remarkable space.

Road Directions

Jct 21a of M6, take M62 to Liverpool City Centre, follow brown 'Cathedrals' signs. From Cheshire, follow signs to Liverpool via Tunnels (tolls applicable), then city centre and 'Cathedrals' signs.

Public Transport Directions
Located in Liverpool City Centre, 10 minutes walk frm Lime Street Station.No 4 'Smart' bus from Paradise Street bus station in the city centre.

## Liverpool Cathedral

St James Mount, Liverpool, Merseyside, L1 7AZ

Tel: +44 (0)151 709 9722

Liverpool Anglican Cathedral is Britain's biggest Cathedral and the 5th largest in Europe. The cathedral is free to enter, however the tower and audio tour is highly recommended. Book tickets through VisitLiverpool by clicking on the 'buy tickets' button to save time!

The Cathedral is a world-class visitor attraction with a full programme of events from Cream Classics music sets to large gala dinners and conferences.

Travel to the top of the tower on the 'Tower Experience' and enjoy unrivalled panoramic views from 500ft above sea level! Here visitors can see the city and way beyond, it's also one of the best places to catch a Mersey sunset.

The Tower Experience includes the Great Space Film on how the cathedral was built (available in 7 languages), a visit to the Bell Chamber - the world's heaviest peal of bells and of course a trip to the top!

The Cathedral also offers a choice of two dining venues. The Mezzanine Cafe inside the Cathedral and the Welsford that even serves a traditional Roast Dinner on a Sunday.

Liverpool Cathedral remain committed to keeping entry free to all, despite receiving no government funding or subsidy

## Liverpool Waterfront

*Liverpool Waterfront is a staple on your places to visit list in Liverpool. It has beauty, it has history, culture, art, music food & drink in a breathtaking and iconic setting.*

Diverse in its appeal the waterfront offers everything from a sing-along in The Beatles Story to a perhaps windy, but picturesque riverside stroll.

Where else could you marvel at truly magnificent mercantile architecture like the famous Liver Building; enjoy world-class contemporary art at Tate Liverpool; visit one of the UK's leading photography spaces, Open Eye Gallery; explore the Merseyside Maritime Museum, visit the International Slavery Museum (the only of its kind to look at aspects of historical and contemporary slavery) and become interactive at the recently opened Museum of Liverpool - all within a stone's throw of one another.

But this would not be a waterfront without the River Mersey, the network of historic docks and the canal link which allows evocative narrow boats to moor right in the heart of Liverpool. Relaxing, of course, but our water is also a place to have fun!

Why not hop aboard a Mersey Ferry for stunning views, fascinating history and unlimited sea air? Or explore the waterfront by bike, taking in the sights and sounds of this world class skyline.

A fantastic array of lively bars, cafes, restaurants and premier hotels offers everything from a quick espresso to a romantic dinner or indeed a huge pizza for all the family to share.

Whether you are planning to visit this impressive UNESCO World Heritage Site for the day or are looking for a family weekend packed full of fun and adventure Liverpool Waterfront won't disappoint.

## Liverpool Architecture

*If you look down just for a moment while walking through Liverpool, chances are you'll miss something amazing. The city is home to a vast number of stunning and historic buildings. It actually houses over 2,500 listed buildings and 27 of these are Grade I.*

The beautiful architecture of Liverpool has a story to tell; it represents over 300 years of a port of worldwide importance, whose fortunes declined in the twentieth century but is now experiencing a renaissance as a cultural capital, hosting world-class events, breaking records and collecting numerous accolades.

The Victorian Albert Dock located on Liverpool's waterfront is the largest single collection of Grade I listed buildings in the UK made entirely out of cast iron, brick and stone. The Albert Dock does not only offer a beautiful backdrop to a quayside stroll, but a wide variety of restaurants, galleries, museums and more to enjoy, including key attractions such as Tate Liverpool, The Beatles Story, the Merseyside Maritime Museum and the International Slavery Museum.

A short walk from The Albert Dock is where you'll find the Three Graces; The Royal Liver Building, The Cunard Building and the Port of Liverpool Building. The Royal Liver Building sports the famous Liver Birds, the mythical creatures which symbolise Liverpool. For nearly a century these buildings have defined one of the world's most recognised skylines, which can be admired from aboard the historic Mersey Ferry.

The Bluecoat is thought to be Liverpool's oldest building in the city centre, dating back to the early 1700s. Visitors can now enjoy a year-round programme of visual art, literature, music and dance here. The Liverpool Town Hall was constructed in the 1700s between 1749 and 1754 and its beautiful interiors are a prime example of late Georgian architecture.

Liverpool's architecture can be seen from another level from the Liverpool Anglican Cathedral tower, the largest cathedral in Britain, taking 74 years to construct from 1904. Look down from this intricate beauty and admire the elegant Georgian townhouses that are always in high demand for filming.

In Liverpool, we don't do things by halves, being home to two cathedrals. Just a short walk away is Hope Street, which connects the two Cathedrals and is where you'll find The Metropolitan Cathedral of Christ the King. This cathedral was originally planned to be a huge structure similar to the neo-gothic Anglican, but due to pressures of war and rising costs the design was abandoned. The cathedral now stands as a modern circular design featuring glorious multi-coloured stained glass windows; completed in 1967 it still features Lutyens Crypt, which was built as part of the original design.

Outside the city centre, Speke Hall dates from the Tudor period, recognisable from its black and white timber appearance. Croxteth Hall also has ties to this era, with one of its wings dating back to 1575 (though the majority of the building was completed in the 18th and 19th centuries).

This is just a brief snapshot of Liverpool's stunning architecture, so when you're walking through the streets of the city, remember to look up because you might miss something beautiful!

## Arts & Culture

Did you know that Liverpool has more museums and galleries than any other UK city outside of the capital? Many of these are also free to enter. The city region also boasts fifteen theatres and halls, ranging from the modern Liverpool M&S Bank Arena to the Art Deco style Philharmonic Hall, home to the Royal Liverpool Philharmonic Orchestra.

The Liverpool Empire Theatre is the second largest theatre in the country and showcases the best in local, national and international talent, often hosting shows direct from London's West End. Liverpool's Royal Court Theatre always guarantees a great night of entertainment, hosting great comedies and musicals throughout the year, with largely local casts and crews.

The Everyman and Playhouse theatres provide an eclectic mix of forward-thinking theatre in great settings, with the Everyman being awarded the RIBA Stirling Prize in 2014 for best new building of the year.

Just 5 minutes from Liverpool's Lime Street Station is the beautiful William Brown Street, where you'll find a delightful cluster of culture including the Walker Art Gallery (the national gallery of the North), World Museum, Liverpool Central Library and St John's Gardens.

Down on the waterfront at Albert Dock is Tate Liverpool, the home of contemporary art in the North, staging major international exhibitions throughout the year.

Then there's the Liverpool Biennial, the international festival dedicated to contemporary art from all over the world, taking place every two years and bringing a number of key pieces of public artwork to the city both during and outside of the festival.

Just a short train or ferry ride away in Wirral is the dainty village of Port Sunlight home of Sunlight Soap and the Lever Brothers. The Lady Lever Art Gallery houses Lord Leverhulme's personal collection, featuring a wide range of fine and decorative arts.

## Museums

*Liverpool has one of the most impressive collections of museums in Europe.*

Opened in 2011 in a landmark waterfront building, the Museum of Liverpool is the UK's first museum dedicated to the history of a city. Visitors can explore how Liverpool's port, its people and its creative, industrial and sporting history have shaped the city.

Many museums and galleries are located around the Albert Dock, such as the Merseyside Maritime Museum and International Slavery Museum, where you can find out all about the companies, people and ships connected to this port city.

St George's Quarter, close to Lime Street station, is home to World Museum, where you can discover treasures from around the world, meet live creatures and explore outer space.

In Wirral, Port Sunlight Museum and Garden Village is a great day out, celebrating the unique heritage of this industrial landmark. You'll also find the Wirral Tramway and Transport Museum - a celebration of Birkenhead's place in the history of public transport.

## Museum Of Liverpool

Pier Head, Liverpool, Merseyside, L3 1DG

Tel: 0151 478 4545

The Museum of Liverpool is the world's first national museum devoted to the history of a regional city and the largest newly-built national museum in Britain for more than a century. In 2018, it will mark 10 years on Liverpool's UNESCO World Heritage Site waterfront and 10 years of representing Liverpool's unique and interesting history.

Hop on board the overhead railway, get up close to the stage where John Lennon and Paul McCartney first met, immerse yourself in the city's rich sporting and creative history and experience for yourself what it means to be Liverpudlian. Don't miss the 360º immersive films about Liverpool and Everton FC and The Beatles!

Exhibits showcase popular culture and tackle social, historical and contemporary issues of Liverpool's region in an accessible, engaging manner.

More than 6,000 objects bring Liverpool's incredible heritage to life, celebrating thousands of years of the city's achievements.

Exhibits include Ben Johnson's Liverpool Cityscape, a life-size Liverbird, the first Ford Anglia from Ford's Halewood production line and Chris Boardman's famous Lotus sport bike. Book a place in Little Liverpool and introduce your youngest children to the wonders of the Museum of Liverpool.

The museum also houses changing exhibits, examples include 'Reel Stories': that explores Liverpool's history on the silver screen and 'Growing up in the city' which s a photographic exhibition exploring a childhood in Liverpool.

Head to the skylight galleries to see the sweeping views of the Three Graces - this window actually won 'Best window with a view' - so is definitely worth a stop off.

The café on the ground floor serves delicious traditional British food with a contemporary twist. Here, you can relax and enjoy excellent views of the canal and Albert Dock. Free Wifi is also available here.

Road Directions

Road access to Merseyside is excellent with the motorway network making access to central areas quick and easy. From the M6 follow the M56 or M62 to Liverpool.

Public Transport Directions

Regular services to and from Liverpool make it one of the most accessible cities on the UK rail network. Virgin trains operate a London-Liverpool service, with a journey time of just over 2 hours. National Express operate regular services from all major towns and cities in Britain to Norton Street Coach Station, Liverpool.

## Merseyside Maritime Museum

Albert Dock, Liverpool, Merseyside, L3 4AQ

Tel: +44 (0)151 478 4499

Submerge yourself in Liverpool's historic seafaring past at the Merseyside Maritime Museum.

Located in the heart of the Albert Dock, it's the ideal location to explore and uncover the development of the world famous port. Boats, paintings, ship models, ship wrecked objects, uniforms and more.

Merseyside Maritime Museum brings Liverpool's nautical history to life. Discover the city's pivotal role as the gateway to the new world.

Highlights include the Life at Sea display, telling the story of the merchant navy. Children and and families can learn about Liverpool's role in The Battle of the Atlantic during World War Two.

Throughout the museum you'll find exhibits, trails and free events perfect for the little ones.

To find out what trails and activities are taking place, just visit the information desk when you arrive and ask a member of the friendly museum team. Here you can also book onto the eye-opening tour of the Old Dock, taking you underground into the world's first commercial enclosed wet dock. During the summer months,

Immerse yourself in the Museum's extensive Maritime archives. See how artists have portrayed the port of Liverpool and the many ships once found on the river Mersey in the Art and the Sea Gallery, and enjoy a changing temporary exhibitions programme.

At the information desk you can also book a tour of the Old Dock, the world's first commercial enclosed wet dock, and during the summer months, the Edmund Gardner pilot ship.

On the 4th floor, enjoy incredible food accompanied by stunning views of the Albert Dock and waterfront at the 2010 Michelin Guide-listed Maritime Dining Room. On the ground floor, the Quayside Café serves lighter bites and refreshments and nearby is the shop for all of your nautical-themed souvenir needs.

Seized! The border and customs uncovered, the national museum of the UK Border Force can be found in the basement, while the International Slavery Museums is on the third floor.

Road Directions

The Maritime Museum is located at the Albert Dock on Liverpool's famous waterfront, adjacent to the Pier Head. Please note that the riverside walkway between

Pier Head and the Albert Dock will be closed while construction takes place in the area.

Public Transport Directions
Located in the Albert Dock complex, the nearest train station is at James Street.

## International Slavery Museum

3rd Floor, Merseyside Maritime Museum, Albert
Dock, Liverpool, Merseyside, L3 4AQ
Tel: 0151 478 4499

The International Slavery Museum is located within Liverpool's Albert Dock, inside the Merseyside Maritime Museum building.

The Museum is the only one of it's kind and looks at the aspects of historical and contemporary slavery. Expect to be taken on a thought-provoking and moving explorative journey beginning at life before slavery. It looks at the people of West Africa and their rich and varied history anbd culture developed, long before European slaves.

At the beginning of the museum, youngsters can explore the Igbo family replica and learn about traditional African Culture.

The story continues to enslavement, of which features a walk-in audio visual display which capturing the horrors and conditions that were endured by slaves on slave ships across the Atlantic. This chapter of the museum is narrated by people that were stripped of their identities and treated as animals by crews.

The final section of the museum looks collects reminders of the racism and discrimination faced by the Black population even after the abolition of the slave trade. However, this is not the end of the exhibition, the museum delves into the spirit shown by people of African descent and how this influenced the societies of culture of America and Europe today.

Visitors are encouraged to to visit the Black Achievers Wall, the Freedom Wall and to visit the Campaign Zone which regularly displays exhibitions on how millions all over the world are still being sold as objects and forced to work for little or no pay.

## World Museum

William Brown Street, Liverpool, Merseyside, L3 8EN

Tel: 0151 478 4393

From the sea to the stars, a visit to World Museum reveals millions of years of the Earth's history through thousands of exhibits and hands-on activities.

Travel to distant continents and ancient civilisations in the amazing galleries.

*The Museum's brand new Ancient Egypt: A journey through time gallery takes visitors on a 5,000-year adventure to the land of the pharaohs, and reveals one of the UK's most significant collections of Egyptian objects. There's no better place to come face-to-face with the past and delve deeper into the myths, mysteries and rituals surrounding the ancient Egyptian afterlife than in the gallery's atmospheric Mummy Room.*

Discover the wonders of the natural world in the award winning Clore Natural History Centre. This is the place to get your hands on more than 20,000 of the most unusual items from the huge collections, from a hippopotamus skull to a mammoth tooth.

There's also the Weston Discovery Centre, which offers a range of activities and interaction to provide a fascinating insight into human history throughout the ages.

Find a rainbow array of beautiful tropical fish at the aquarium, expert staff are on hand to answer questions and run demonstrations in which visitors can observe and learn more about live marine creatures .Get closer than you ever thought possible to creepy crawlies at the bug house. The bug house displays a selection of specimens from the museum's vast research collection alongside real live colonies of leaf cutter ants.

Blast off into space at World Museum's Planetarium with some brand new shows. Meet IQ, Scooter and Nat in *Fly me to the Moon*, a fantastic adventure for young space fans aged four and over. Or, join Coyote in a fast-paced, fun show that explores lunar phases, eclipses and other puzzles in *Earth, Moon and Sun,* aimed at visitors aged six and over. Buy your tickets at the information desk on your visit.

*Don't forget to complete your day with a relaxing visit to the Museum's brand new café and shop facilities.*

Road Directions

Follow the brown and white road signs for central Liverpool attractions and Walker Art Gallery Look out for signs for St John's or Queen Square car parks. These are between the main shopping area bus stops and St John's Gardens (behind St George's Hall). World Museum Liverpool is on the other side of St John's Gardens.

Public Transport Directions

Regular services to and from Liverpool make it one of the most accessible cities on the UK rail network. Virgin trains operate a London-Liverpool service, with a journey time of just over 2 hours. National Express operate regular services from all major towns and cities in Britain to Norton Street Coach Station, Liverpool. www.merseytravel.gov.uk has comprehensive transport information and a 'Journey Planner' service or you can call Traveline on 0871 200 22 33.

## Port Sunlight Museum & Garden Village

23 King George's Drive, Port Sunlight, Wirral, CH62 5DX

Tel: +44 (0)151 644 6466

Discover more than a century of rich history at Port Sunlight Museum, located in the heart of the model village in Wirral.

The award-winning museum tells the story of 'soap king' William Hesketh Lever, his great vision for the village and the lives of the people who lived and worked in Port Sunlight.

The museum celebrates the unique heritage of the village, encompassing its formal planning, architecture and parks & gardens, from its foundation in 1888 to life in the village today.

For those wanting to explore the village, the museum offers a variety of tour options. Choose from a multimedia tour, guided village tour led by a Port Sunlight guide or a self-guided walking trail taking you on a circular route starting and ending at the museum. The museum is filled with a mix of special exhibitions, evolving displays, interactive touch screens and film footage from past into present day; in addition to a recently restored Edwardian restored worker's cottage.

Refreshments are available from a contemporary tea room located above the museum, open daily, the tea room caters for individuals and small groups (large groups must pre-book) serving a delicious selection of freshly prepared sandwiches, light lunches, award-winning cakes. Offering a full yearly programme of events, Port Sunlight Museum is a great day out for couples, families and groups.

## Road Directions

By Car: Leave the M53 at junction 4, follow the B5137 and take the second left onto the B5136 towards Port Sunlight. Follow the brown and white road signs for Port Sunlight Village.

## Public Transport Directions

By train: The nearest train station is Bebington although Port Sunlight is also within walking distance. They are both on the Chester and Ellesmere Port Merseyrail lines. Leave the station and come out onto Old Chester Road (use the ramp if you require level access). Turn left, cross at the traffic lights, then turn left again down Bebington Road, passing under the railway bridge. Turn next right down Greendale Road. Continue along the pavement on the same side as the cottages for approximately 400 yards until you see the

Leverhulme memorial Take the pathway on your left leading into Windy Bank. The entrance to Port Sunlight Museum is to the left of the fountain.

By bus: Take number 464 to Bebington Road bus stop (starts at Sir Thomas Street in Liverpool city centre) or number 38 to Bebington rail station bus stop (runs between Clatterbridge Hospital and West Kirby station). Once you get off the bus refer to the above directions from Bebington railway station.

## Wirral Tramway & Wirral Transport Museum
1 Taylor Street, Birkenhead, Merseyside, CH41 1BG
Tel: 0151 647 2128
Come and enjoy the sights and sounds of yesteryear at the Wirral Transport Museum, where the volunteers of the Merseyside Tramway Preservation Society restore and preserve transport of the past for the delight and benefit of the present and the future.

Take a ride back in time on one of our electric heritage trams and let the memories of a bygone age come flooding back.

As you wander through our fascinating collection of trams, buses, cars, motorcycles and cycles, see the delight on your children's faces as they gaze in wonder on the miniature world of our model railway, while you explore the vast array of transport and other fascinating memorabilia.

There's so much to see so much to enjoy and now, thanks to the support of Wirral Borough Council, so much more. For, following the completion of a substantial refurbishment programme in the Spring of 2018, we can now offer our visitors much improved facilities such as a new separate foyer and entrance, a tea room, sales kiosk (formed from two former Victorian Mersey Ferry booths), a suite of toilets, including for those with mobility or other physical issues, a lift to the second level, leading to a new Viewing Gallery and new or improved displays.

There really is something for everyone and we pride ourselves in the warmth of our welcome and the friendliness of our volunteers.

Road Directions

By road: Follow "All Docks" exit off the M53 and take the A5139 to next traffic island. Turn right following brown tourist signs for Mersey Ferries. Continue along Tower Road, turn left at next roundabout along Canning Street and take the first right.

Public Transport Directions

Nearest Railway Station: HamiltonSquareBoard the Tram at Woodside Ferry terminalFor further public transport information please contact Merseytravel on 0871 200 22

# Galleries

*Liverpool has an impressive collection of galleries, from traditional to contemporary. Take your pick.*

Tate Liverpool needs no introduction it stages major international exhibitions of modern art, featuring work by everyone from Tracey Emin to Picasso.

In the beautiful William Brown Street, you can find Walker Art Gallery, the national gallery of the North, which houses works by Hockney, Degas, Turner and Rembrandt.

Check out The Bluecoat too, the distinctive Grade I listed, 300-year-old arts centre which offers a lively programme of visual art, music, dance, live art and literature.

Open Eye Gallery is an independent not-for-profit photography gallery championing photography as an art form and staging challenging and entertaining exhibitions.

FACT, the Foundation for Art and Creative Technology, in addition to its cinema screens, shows ground-breaking new media art exhibitions.

The Atkinson is Southport's home for music, theatre, art, poetry, literature and history, right in the middle of Lord Street.

And across the River Mersey at Port Sunlight in Wirral is the Lady Lever Art Gallery, a beautiful, highly personal art collection of fine and decorative arts. Definitely worth crossing the river for.

Liverpool city region is also home to world-class public art, including the awe-inspiring Another Place at Crosby Beach, the 100 cast-iron life-size sculptures of Angel of the North artist Antony Gormley staring out to sea.

## Tate Liverpool

Albert Dock, Liverpool, Merseyside, L3 4BB

Tel: +44 (0)151 702 7400

Welcome to the home of British and international modern and contemporary art in the North; Tate Liverpool. Aren't we lucky?

Since its opening at the spectacular Grade I listed Albert Dock in 1988, Tate Liverpool has become one of the most visited art galleries outside of London. Its close proximity to the city centre by foot and the sheer amount of special exhibitions it hosts every year make it a must-see stop on your visit to Liverpool.

Bringing together artworks from all over the world, Tate Liverpool prides itself on staging an ever-evolving programme of unique and incredible collections. With past artists featured including Gustav Klimt, Pablo Picasso, Andy Warhol and Claude Monet, we're always looking forward to what the next Tate Liverpool season will bring to our doorstep.

Tate Liverpool's gallery offers large displays of work from the National Collection free of charge. The Collection features the work of artists including L.S. Lowry, Cindy Sherman, Louise Bourgeois Mamelles and Glenn Ligon, making Tate Liverpool the perfect place to visit your favourite artworks, as well as discovering something completely new.

But why stop at the displays and exhibitions? Tate Liverpool holds frequent special events, like talks and workshops for you to exclusively delve into the exhibitions, as well as family activities, like creating your very own comics. Taking a break won't be hard either, with magnificent views across the Albert Dock at the cafe.

Take home a piece of your day with the souvenirs at the the Tate Shop; find jewellery, art materials and designer homewares, along with gifts, books and postcards which will make your friends back home wish that they came with you. Got a student card? You're in luck. You'll get a 10% discount on all purchases!

However you choose to experience the gallery, Tate Liverpool is the perfect place to relax, be inspired and have fun. Come and see.

Public Transport Directions

On Foot: Approaching from the Strand, turn onto the Salthouse Dock opposite the Hilton Hotel. Continue straight on passing the Pumphouse Inn on the right and the Maritime Museum on the left. The quickest route to us is across the Hartley Bridge. This bridge can sometimes be closed to pedestrians with very little notice to allow boats into the Albert Dock. These closures are generally only for a short time.

On Bike: Bike racks are located in the Mermaid Courtyard, adjacent to Tate Liverpool.

By Bus: Liverpool ONE Bus Station on Canning Street is directly opposite the Albert Dock, approximately 365 metres from Tate Liverpool. Route C4 also stops at the Albert Dock.

By Train: The nearest train station to Tate Liverpool is James Street station, Liverpool L27PQ (720 metres approx.). Mainline rail tickets to Liverpool Lime Street station are valid for travel to James Street Station.

Liverpool Lime Street will be closed 30 September 22 October 2017 for improvements to the station.

By Ferry: Mersey Ferries from Seacombe and Woodside on the Wirral call at the Pier Head (960 metres approx.). Access from the Pier Head to the gallery is via The Strand.

By Car: To get to Tate Liverpool, follow the brown signs to the Waterfront. The following car parks are near Tate Liverpool:

Next to Echo Arena is the Liverpool Waterfront Car Park, a multi-storey car park with 1,600 secure, covered spaces open 24/7.

Q-Park Liverpool ONE, with 2,000 underground spaces: 35 Strand Street, Liverpool L1 8LT. Visitors to Tate Liverpool can park at Q Park and receive a 50% discount on parking for up to 24 hours. Ask for a voucher from a member of staff when visiting the gallery.

By Coach: Coach parking is available at the Kings Dock Car and Coach Park, near to Tate Liverpool. More information for drivers www.albertdock.com.

By Shopmobility: Visitors may also like to make use of Liverpool's Shopmobility service, on the third floor of the Liverpool ONE shopping centre.

## Lady Lever Art Gallery

Port Sunlight Village, Port Sunlight, Merseyside, CH62 5EQ

Tel: 0151 478 4136

The Lady Lever Art Gallery is regarded as one of the finest art galleries in Europe. It's located in model village, Port Sunlight in Wirral, a place rich in architectural charm.

The gallery was founded by William Hesketh Lever (1851-1925) and is dedicated to his wife Elizabeth, Lady Lever. Lever wanted to share his collections with the public and the works on display at the gallery have been personally selected.

Inside the gallery, visitors will find the best of Lever's personal art collection and the finest collection of Wedgwood jasperware anywhere in the world. The Pre-Raphaelite painting collection is internationally renowned and features works by Millais, Rossetti, Burne-Jones and Holman Hunt.

For younger visitors, the activity rooms are an interactive space where they can get hands-on and have fun with crafts, dressing up and story telling.

Lady Lever often houses temporary exhibitions and popular free events, be sure to check the site before visiting.

Road Directions

From Liverpool: Go through the Birkenhead (Queensway) Tunnel (£1.40 toll for cars, £4.20 for coaches). Once you leave the tunnel follow signs for Port Sunlight, driving along A41(New Chester Road) - the gallery is sign posted all the way from the tunnel and situated opposite Port Sunlight Museum.

From elsewhere: Leave the M53 at junction 4, follow the B5137 and take the second left onto the B5136 towards Port Sunlight. Follow the brown and white road signs for Port Sunlight Village. Once you are in the village follow the signs for Lady Lever Art Gallery.

Public Transport Directions

By Train: The nearest station is Bebington although Port Sunlight is also within walking distance. They are both on the Chester and Ellesmere Port Merseyrail lines. Leave the station and come out onto Old Chester Road (use the ramp if you require level access). Turn left, cross at the traffic lights, then turn left again down Bebington Road, passing under the railway bridge. Turn next right down Greendale Road. Continue along the pavement on the same side as the cottages for approximately 400 yards until you see the Leverhulme memorial and the Lady Lever Art Gallery on your left. Take the pathway on your left leading into Windy Bank and towards the memorial and the gallery. The entrance to the gallery is to the right side of the building opposite the fountain.

By bus: Take number 464 to Bebington Road bus stop (starts at Sir Thomas Street in Liverpool city centre) or number 38 to Bebington rail station bus stop (runs between Clatterbridge Hospital and West Kirby station). Once you get off the bus refer to the above directions from Bebington railway station.

## Riba North

Mann Island, Liverpool, Merseyside, L3 1BP

Tel: +44 (0)151 703 0107

RIBA North is the Royal Institute of British Architects' National Architecture Centre on Liverpool's Waterfront. The centre was opened in June 2017 and was recently awarded the title of 'Best Newcomer to the Visitor Economy' at the Liverpool City Region Tourism Awards 2018. It is situated in extremely close proximity to the Open Eye Gallery and Museum of Liverpool, a stone's throw from the Albert Dock.

RIBA North is a place for everyone to discover more about architecture and is an inspirational resource for both RIBA members and the public. Through exhibitions, events and walking tours the centre champions architects, architecture and good design.

At the heart of RIBA North is the City Gallery, a space for visitors to learn more about Liverpool's past, present and future, as well as the processes involved in urban development and the evolution of the built environment.

RIBA North's City Gallery includes the Digital City Model, an interactive 3D model that tells a variety of stories about Liverpool and the surrounding area. It is also an extraordinary professional tool, which can be used by developers, architects and planners to host public consultations, anticipate the impact of future development and encourage the best design approaches.

The centre is also home to an RIBA shop, selling all manner of different architectural inspired gifts for children and adults, a showcase of Northern designers and RIBA merchandise, and a fantastic selection of books along with architects tools of the trade.

We have step free access to the main entrance and step free access to the first floor via a lift located at the rear of the ground floor café. We also welcome guide dogs. If you have any questions about access, or if you have any special requirements, please contact us before your visit.

RIBA North is also home to a programme of architectural walking tours of Liverpool. The six tours cover five of Liverpool's UNESCO World Heritage areas and during the Summer season run five days per week. These are bookable in advance through the RIBA North site. Tours last approximately two hours and whether you a city resident or visiting Liverpool from elsewhere, you will discover the history of Liverpool through its key buildings and public spaces. The award-winning

RIBA volunteer guides will tell the story of Liverpool's past, present and future.

Road Directions

Located on the A 5039 From the motorways follow brown signs for the Waterfront / Albert Dock

Public Transport Directions

Train Liverpool Lime Street 20 minute walk Liverpool James Street (Wirral Line) 2 minute walk Moorfields (Wirral Line and Northern Line) 5 minute walk    Bus Liverpool ONE Bus Station 8 minute walk For full details about local bus and train services please visit merseytravel.gov.uk   Ferry Pier Head Ferry Terminal 2 minute walk For full details about ferry services please visit merseyferries.co.uk    Coach Liverpool ONE Bus Station (National Express) 8 minute walk For information about coach drop-off and pick-up facilities please visit visitliverpool.com   Car parking Q-Park at Liverpool ONE, The Strand, Liverpool L1 8LT 8 minute walk Two dedicated blue badge parking spaces are located on Brunswick Street 5 minute walk

## Sudley House

Mossley Hill Road, Mossley Hill, Liverpool,

Merseyside, L18 8BX

Tel: 0151 478 4016

Experience the magnificent art collection of Victorian merchant ship owner George Holt in the heart of suburban Liverpool, at Sudley House. A treasure trove of masterpieces await you by artists including Millais, Rossetti, Burne-Jones, Turner, Romney, Gainsborough and Landseer, forming the only merchant art collection in the UK still in its original setting. A series of temporary exhibitions are hosted by Sudley House each year featuring costume and contemporary works.

Audio-visual displays on the ground floor recreate Victorian family life and younger visitors are welcome to enjoy the activities and in the Childhood room. Visitors of all ages will enjoy the recently refurbished and extended tea room and the beautiful grounds in which Sudley House is set.

Sudley House has limited on-site parking, free WIFI in the café and is a ten minute walk from Mossley Hill Station.

Road Directions
Exit the M62 jct 4, turn left onto Queens Drive. Follow Queens Drive till the end. Turn left onto Mossley Hill Rd continue across Rose Lane. The Entrance for Sudley House will be on your Right.

Public Transport Directions
Mossley Hill Train Station is 0.6 miles from Sudley Houes.For public transport information please contact Merseytravel.

## Walker Art Gallery

William Brown Street, Liverpool, Merseyside, L3 8EL
Tel: +44 (0)151 478 4199
The Walker Art Gallery holds a stunning collection of paintings, sculpture and decorative arts spanning over six hundred years. Home to outstanding works by Rubens, Rembrandt, Poussin and Gainsborough, the Walker is also one of the finest art galleries in Europe.

Here you'll also find Tudor portraits and a large collection of Victorian and Pre-Raphaelite works including Dante's Dream by Rossetti, hanging alongside other artists such as Millais, Turner, Monet and Holman Hunt.

Don't miss the Walker's collection of 20th century modern and contemporary art that includes pieces by Lucien Freud, Bridget Riley and Henry Moore. The Gallery also exhibits the current and past winners of the John Moores Painting Prize, the oldest painting competition in the UK. Look out for work by David Hockney, Peter Doig, Martin Green and 2012 winner, Sarah Pickstone.

The Decorative Arts gallery contains over 500 pieces of ceramics, glass, pottery, fashion and furniture from the ancient world to the 20th century.

For families with younger children, there is Big Art for Little Artists, a specially designed gallery created for children under 8 years old. Add to this to a welcoming café with free Wifi and a gift shop stocking prints, jewellery, cards, books and other souvenirs, you have the perfect art lover's day out. The Walker Art Gallery is a three minute walk from Lime Street Station.

**Road Directions**

The Walker is a short walk from Liverpool Lime Street station. Leave the station via the exit closest to the ticket office turning left along Lime Street, past the Empire Theatre. Head towards the fountain via the pedestrian crossing. The Walker Art Gallery is the second building along, directly behind the fountain. The nearest local line train station is Liverpool Lime Street lower level, however this is only served by Wirral Line trains. The Walker is within walking distance of the bus stations at Queen Square and the Paradise Street Interchange. From Queen Square: keep the Queen Square Centre and

The Royal Court Theatre on your right and walk towards St George's Hall and the adjoining gardens. Cross at the pedestrian lights, turn left and walk through the gardens, keeping the back of St George's Hall to your right. As you leave the gardens you will see a fountain across to your right. The fountain is directly in front of the gallery. From Paradise Street: leave the bus station by the eastern exit (the end furthest from the river and the Albert Dock) and before you reach the traffic lights go left through a pedestrianised shopping area (by John Lewis). Pass several shops, cross the junction with Lord/Church Street and progress along Whitechapel. Take the pavement on the right side of the road, passing a taxi rank, bus station and several pubs. Cross the road towards St Johns Gardens, and keeping the gardens on your right follow the path round to the right. Go past World Museum Liverpool and the gallery is at the top of the road on the left.

**Public Transport Directions**
The Walker is a short walk from Liverpool Lime Street station - Liverpool's mainline train station. Simply leave the concourse via the exit closest to the ticket office

(this route is also suitable for those requiring level access) . You come out on Lord Nelson Street, facing the side of the Empire Theatre. Turn left out onto Lime Street (St George's Hall is opposite). Go right along Lime Street, past the Empire Theatre.

Cross Lime Street at the pedestrian crossing near the theatre (going towards the fountain), and walk onto William Brown Street. The Walker is the second building along, directly behind the fountain. The nearest local line train station is Liverpool Lime Street lower level, however this is only served by Wirral Line trains. The Walker is within walking distance of the bus stations at Queen Square and the Paradise Street Interchange. From Queen Square: keep the Queen Square Centre and

The Royal Court Theatre on your right and walk towards St George's Hall and the adjoining gardens. Cross at the pedestrian lights, turn left and walk through the gardens, keeping the back of St George's Hall to your right. As you leave the gardens you will see a fountain across to your right. The fountain is directly in front of the gallery. From Paradise Street: leave the bus station by the eastern exit (the end furthest from the river and the Albert Dock) and before you reach the traffic lights go left through a pedestrianised shopping area (by John Lewis).

Pass several shops, cross the junction with Lord/Church Street and progress along Whitechapel. Take the pavement on the right side of the road, passing a taxi rank, bus station and several pubs. Cross the road towards St Johns Gardens, and keeping the gardens on your right follow the path round to the right. Go past World Museum Liverpool and the gallery is at the top of the road on the left.

## Chapel Gallery

St Helens Rd, Ormskirk, L39 4QR

Tel: 01695 571 328

The Chapel Gallery's programme includes internationally regarded artists, such as David Hockney and Peter Blake, while bringing innovative contemporary art and craft from across the UK to the region.

Alongside the Gallery, Chapel Gallery is also home to a Café and a Craft & Design Shop, so you can explore the exhibitions, get creative, then browse the Shop and relax with a coffee and cake at the Café, and with their new award winning caterer that will be a delight.

The gallery is situated on the ground floor and is fully accessible to disabled visitors. Groups larger than ten should contact the Gallery staff. Opening Times - Every Tuesday - Saturday 10:00am - 4:30pm. Closed Sundays and Mondays.

**The Atkinson**

The Atkinson, Lord Street, Southport, Merseyside, PR8 1DB

Tel: +44(0) 1704 533333

The Atkinson is Southport's home for music, theatre, art, literature and history. You can find us in the middle of the iconic Lord Street and just 3 minutes' walk from Southport train station.

We offer an exciting and varied destination for families, cultural tourists and arts enthusiasts alike, with a full day and night time offer. Significant investment has been made in refurbishing our stunning 19th century buildings to create a welcoming and accessible multi art-form venue with a strong contemporary feel.

Our traditional Theatre and dynamic Studio space present an outstanding programme of music, comedy and performing arts from some of the UK's foremost musicians, actors, performers and companies.

The Atkinson is also home to an impressive collection holding over 3,500 artworks and over 25,000 pieces of social history, which are displayed on rotation across our museum and galleries.

The regularly changing exhibition programme presents work from our collection as well as contemporary art, family friendly and thematic exhibitions delivered in partnership with other cultural organisations.

Our Egyptology Gallery presents the Goodison Egyptology Collection, where families can discover what life was like in ancient Egypt at the time of the Pharaohs. The collection was unseen for over 40 years until 2014 when Heritage Lottery Funding provided an exciting interactive gallery for it to be displayed in.

Explore the history of those who have lived and worked along the Sefton coast, from prehistoric times to the present day in our museum Between Land and Sea 10,000 Years of Sefton's Coast.

Find a range of handmade items from local artists, local history information and museum & exhibition souvenirs in The Atkinson's shop. We regularly host craft fairs and are always showcasing items from local makers.

Relax in our award-winning café A Great Little Place and enjoy great coffee and delicious fresh food. The café offers the finest locally-roasted artisan coffee delivered by trained baristas and imaginative food created in our own kitchens.

The Atkinson is also home to Southport Library who offer a range of services to the local community as well as tourist information.

The Atkinson is open throughout the year and presents a varied seasonal programme and changing exhibitions, events and lectures, so whatever time of year you visit, we offer a fun, creative and varied day out with family or friends.

**Road Directions**
ith a variety of road networks leading into Southport taking in some stunning views, it is easy to travel to Southport by car:

From the South, take the M6 to exit 26; the M58 will take you to Ormskirk and then take the A570 to Southport.

From the North, follow the A59 from Preston (exit 31 from the M6) and then follow the signs to Southport.

## Parking

There is on-road pay and display parking around Southport as well as a number of off-road car parks. For more detailed car parking information in Southport please visit Sefton site for car parking information

## Disabled Parking

There is more information on our accessibility page. There is disabled parking at the front of the building that is available but is limited to two spaces. These spaces are offered on a first come, first served basis. We will provide a 'The Atkinson Visitor Parking Permit' for three hours for the first two visitors who require them. These can be issued to any visitors who are blue badge holders. The permits are available from the Box Office/shop counter (Call 0151 934 2179) and we do ask for them to be returned at the end of the visit.

## Public Transport Directions
By Train

It could not be easier to visit The Atkinson by Train as Southport station is just 3 minutes walk from the venue.

Merseyrail run fast and frequent services between Liverpool South Parkway (for Liverpool John Lennon Airport), Liverpool City Centre and Southport. You can plan your journey straight to our door with their journey planner application and as we are the last stop on the line it is easy to find us!

Northern Rail operates regular services to Southport from Manchester Airport, Manchester (Piccadilly, Oxford Road, and Victoria stations), Bolton and Wigan. Connecting services to / from the North East and Yorkshire are available at Manchester Piccadilly and from the North, Scotland and the South at Wigan.

By Bus

With a network of travel centres across Merseyside, Merseytravel operate a number of bus services to and from Southport.

National Express coaches serve Southport from all major UK towns and cities making the town easily accessibly by coach.

## Victoria Gallery & Museum

Ashton Street, University of Liverpool, Liverpool, Merseyside, L69 3DR

Tel: 0151 794 2348

Housed in the iconic red-brick Victoria building the Victoria Gallery & Museum is a piece of art in itself.

The beautifully renovated gothic building houses the University of Liverpool's amazing collection of fine art, silver, furniture, sculpture, ceramics, fossils, scientific equipment, zoological specimens collected by and donated to the University throughout its history.

Spanning the 16th to 21st centuries, the art collection comprises more than 6,500 items of fine art, sculpture, furniture, ceramics, glass and silverware.

Some of the highlights of the Museum collection include X-rays from the very beginning of X-ray technology, an early 20th century dental surgery and dinosaur footprints from the North West!

Road Directions
From the M62: at the end of the motorway continue straight ahead on to Edge Lane (A5080 and A5047) and follow the signs for Liverpool city centre and the University.

Parking is avilable in th eUniveristy Visitor car parks.There is a charge for visitor parking. Rates are as displayed in the car parks.

Public Transport Directions
The VG&M is situated at the top of Brownlow Hill in the Victoria Building, with its distinctive red-brick and clock tower. It is a short walk from the city centre.

By rail- The nearest mainline station is Liverpool Lime Street. The nearest local station is Liverpool Central.

By bus - From the City Centre buses 14 and 79 go up Brownlow Hill approximately every 5 minutes. The buses leave from the side of the Adelphi Hotel at the bottom of Brownlow Hill and stop outside the Victoria Gallery & Museum at the top of Brownlow Hill.

## Williamson Art Gallery & Museum

Williamson Art Gallery & Museum, Slatey Road, Birkenhead, Merseyside, CH43 4UE

Tel: 0151 666 3537

Located outside the centre of Birkenhead, the Williamson Art Gallery stands at the core of the Wirral Museums Service, offering more space than any other in its purpose-built galleries.

The Williamson houses one of the best art collections in the North West of England in its beautifully proportioned galleries. Paintings of all sorts, especially British watercolours and work by local artists, join highlights of the decorative arts collections like Liverpool Porcelain and Birkenhead's own contribution to the Arts & Crafts Movement, the Della Robbia Pottery.

Always on show is the largest single display of ship models in the area, focusing on Cammell Laird shipbuilders and their contribution to marine history, the Mersey Ferries and the variety of vessels that used the River Mersey when it was at its busiest.

In addition to the permanent collection a great effort is put into sustaining a spirited programme of temporary exhibitions. Here too the emphasis is on a celebration of the local art scene, but work is also drawn from outside to showcase the best and present it in this outstanding environment. Also the Williamson has built a regional reputation for the quality and variety of its shows.

## The Bluecoat

School Lane, Liverpool, Merseyside, L1 3BX

Tel: 0151 702 5324. Fax: 0151 707 0048

A Grade I listed, 300 year old building in the heart of Liverpool's city centre, the Bluecoat offers a year-round programme of visual art, literature, music, dance and live art.

In addition, the Bluecoat is home to a wide range of artists and creative businesses, ranging from jewellery and ceramic ware at the internationally recognised Display Centre, to hand-made accessories, boutique clothing and specialist hand-engraving and silversmith services.

Visitors to the Bluecoat are welcome to engage in exhibitions, participate in performances, relax in the tranquil garden with a coffee and a cake from our Espresso bar, or indulge in a delicious, locally sourced meal in the beautiful Upstairs bistro.

The Bluecoat offers something for all the family the garden, courtyard and galleries are the perfect place to bring your little ones to explore (and baby changing facilities are available).

Explore our free art Saturday activities for all the family, or take our heritage trail and learn more about the Bluecoat's history.

## Open Eye Gallery

19 Mann Island, Liverpool Waterfront, Liverpool, Merseyside, L3 1BP

Tel: +44 (0)151 236 6768

Founded in 1977 Open Eye Gallery is an independent not-for-profit photography gallery based in Liverpool. One of the UK's leading photography spaces, Open Eye Gallery is the only gallery dedicated to photography and related media in the North West of England.

Open Eye Gallery has consistently championed photography as an art form that is relevant to everyone. It promotes the practice, enjoyment and understanding of photography by creating challenging and entertaining opportunities to experience and appreciate distinctive, innovative photographs.

Open Eye Gallery is located in Mann Island at the heart of the regenerated Waterfront next to the Museum of Liverpool and a stone's throw from Tate Liverpool and Albert Dock.

As well as presenting a programme of international, high-quality exhibitions Open Eye Gallery houses a permanent Archive containing photographs dating from the 1930s to the present day. The gallery also commissions Wall Works - large- scale graphic art installations for the external facade of the gallery.

**Road Directions**
Follow the brown signs to the Waterfront. The nearest multi-storey car park is Q-Park at Liverpool ONE, 35 Strand Street, Liverpool, L1 8LT. There are six blue badge parking spaces about 40 metres from the entrance to the gallery. They are opposite the entrance to the Museum of Liverpool, beside the Great Western Railway building. The spaces need to be pre-booked by calling 0151 478 4545.

**Public Transport Directions**

well as Edward Burne-Jones' monumental watercolour Sponsa de Libano, which stands at more than three metres high.

The exhibition looks at the full breadth of Victorian art by exploring four key themes: Victorian romantics; painters of the Ancient World; the outside world; and late 19th century symbolists.

**Road Directions**

The Walker is a short walk from Liverpool Lime Street station. Leave the station via the exit closest to the ticket office turning left along Lime Street, past the Empire Theatre. Head towards the fountain via the pedestrian crossing. The Walker Art Gallery is the second building along, directly behind the fountain. The nearest local line train station is Liverpool Lime Street lower level, however this is only served by Wirral Line trains.

The Walker is within walking distance of the bus stations at Queen Square and the Paradise Street Interchange. From Queen Square: keep the Queen

Square Centre and The Royal Court Theatre on your right and walk towards St George's Hall and the adjoining gardens. Cross at the pedestrian lights, turn left and walk through the gardens, keeping the back of St George's Hall to your right. As you leave the gardens you will see a fountain across to your right. The fountain is directly in front of the gallery.

From Paradise Street: leave the bus station by the eastern exit (the end furthest from the river and the Albert Dock) and before you reach the traffic lights go left through a pedestrianised shopping area (by John Lewis). Pass several shops, cross the junction with Lord/Church Street and progress along Whitechapel. Take the pavement on the right side of the road, passing a taxi rank, bus station and several pubs. Cross the road towards St Johns Gardens, and keeping the gardens on your right follow the path round to the right. Go past World Museum Liverpool and the gallery is at the top of the road on the left.

**Public Transport Directions**

The Walker is a short walk from Liverpool Lime Street station - Liverpool's mainline train station. Simply leave the concourse via the exit closest to the ticket office (this route is also suitable for those requiring level access) . You come out on Lord Nelson Street, facing the side of the Empire Theatre. Turn left out onto Lime Street (St George's Hall is opposite). Go right along Lime Street, past the Empire Theatre.

Cross Lime Street at the pedestrian crossing near the theatre (going towards the fountain), and walk onto William Brown Street. The Walker is the second building along, directly behind the fountain. The nearest local line train station is Liverpool Lime Street lower level, however this is only served by Wirral Line trains. The Walker is within walking distance of the bus stations at Queen Square and the Paradise Street Interchange.

From Queen Square: keep the Queen Square Centre and The Royal Court Theatre on your right and walk towards St George's Hall and the adjoining gardens.

Cross at the pedestrian lights, turn left and walk through the gardens, keeping the back of St George's Hall to your right. As you leave the gardens you will see a fountain across to your right. The fountain is directly in front of the gallery. From Paradise Street: leave the bus station by the eastern exit (the end furthest from the river and the Albert Dock) and before you reach the traffic lights go left through a pedestrianised shopping area (by John Lewis).

Pass several shops, cross the junction with Lord/Church Street and progress along Whitechapel. Take the pavement on the right side of the road, passing a taxi rank, bus station and several pubs. Cross the road towards St Johns Gardens, and keeping the gardens on your right follow the path round to the right. Go past World Museum Liverpool and the gallery is at the top of the road on the left.

## Royal Liver Building 360

Royal Liver Building, Liverpool, L3 1HU

Tel: +44(0)151 236 4753

For the first time in its 100+ year history, Royal Liver Building is unlocking its doors to the public and inviting you to explore its iconic history with a fully immersive experience.

As one of the stunning 'Three Graces' on Liverpool's waterfront, Royal Liver Building 360 is a must-see attraction. Start your journey at the lower ground floor visitor centre and learn about the building's history as well as its place in Liverpool's heritage. After you've viewed the exhibitions join your guided tour to the tenth and fifteenth floors to enjoy spectacular 360° views of the Liverpool skyline and experience a world-class digital projection show inside the historic clock tower.

**Public Transport Directions**
The Royal Liver Building is based on the Pier Head, Liverpool Waterfront. The main entrance to the attraction is located on Water Street, just off Canada Boulevard.

Please follow signs to the Waterfront, Albert Dock, Mersey Ferries and Pier Head. There is limited on-street parking around the attraction. We are serviced by a range of public and private car parks across the waterfront (please note that we have no affiliation to any car park operators).

## Theatres

*Liverpool theatre has a fantastically strong reputation, and Liverpool city region has plenty of top theatre performance spaces.*

The legendary Everyman and Playhouse theatres are responsible for launching the career of several celebrated actors including Bill Nighy, Julie Walters and the late, great Pete Postlethwaite. They offer an eclectic programme of theatre and frequently stage world premieres by local and international writers.

The Empire is the largest theatre in Liverpool and stages the big musicals and spectacular shows, often straight from the West End.

The Royal Court offers a range of long-running plays and one-off nights from the likes of Joan Rivers, Russell Howard, Dylan Moran, and Ben Elton.

The intimate Unity Theatre, described as 'the most ambitious theatre in Liverpool' by The Guardian, is a hotbed of new and local talent and provides a valuable platform for small theatre companies.

In Wirral, the Floral Pavilion offers theatre, family shows, ballet, ice shows and music in their historical venue on New Brighton waterfront dating from 1913. Southport also has a number of theatre and performance spaces,

## The Capstone Theatre

Liverpool Hope University Creative Campus, 17 Shaw Street, Liverpool, Merseyside, L6 1HP

Tel: 0151 291 3578

Since opening in March 2010, The Capstone Theatre has staged concerts and performances by leading national and international musicians and artists, including Courtney Pine, Kathryn Tickell, Martin Simpson, Kathryn Williams, Chilly Gonzales, Portico Quartet, Harold Budd, The Necks, Arthur Jeffes, Roger Eno, Darius Brubeck Quartet, King Creosote and Jon Hopkins, Martin Taylor and Martin Simpson, Neil Cowley Trio, Dennis Rollins Velocity Trio, Terry Seabrooke's Milestones, Bulbs, Phronesis, Public Service Broadcasting, Lighthouse, Jim Moray, Stacey Kent, Dean Friedman, Eduardo Niebla, Ian Boddy, Berta Rojas and The Smith Quartet, alongside concerts by some of the best local musicians, spoken word events, radio broadcasts, plays, dance performances and film screenings.

The Capstone is part of Liverpool Hope University's Creative Campus that comprises of a vibrant music department with strong links to the Royal Liverpool Philharmonic Orchestra. The department also organises the yearly Cornerstone Festival (November–December).

The Campus also plays host to Milapfest, the UK's leading Indian Arts Development Trust, whose work aims to make a difference to people's lives through inspirational performances and educational experiences. Alongside regular Music and Dance performances at The Capstone, Milapfest organise a series of free monthly concerts 'Music for the Mind and Soul' on the last Saturday afternoon of each month.

**Road Directions**
From the M62:

At the end of the M62, exit straight ahead (signposted A5080 City Centre). Follow Edge Lane Drive to Edge Lane (A5047) and continue on until you see a sign indicating left (for Universities). Go left and then right onto the A5047 Irvine Street, leading to Pembroke Place. Go right at the traffic lights into Anson Street, then right again on to London Road and take the left hand lane turning into Moss Street. At next lights proceed straight on to Shaw Street. The venue is approx. 100 yards on the left hand side.

From the M56:

From Junction 15 join the M53. Continue to Liverpool via the Wallasey Tunnel (Kingsway). Exit straight ahead toward Scotland Road/Byrom Street. Keep in the left-hand lane and at the traffic lights follow to left (signposted Warrington, Manchester and M62) on to New Islington. Stay in the left-hand lane to the second set of traffic lights and turn left on to Shaw Street. The venue is approx. 100 yards on the left hand side.

**Public Transport Directions**
Bus:

From Liverpool City centre (Queen Square) the buses which go near to the Creative Campus are the 12, 13, 14, 14a, 14b and 19a which stop on Islington near Staples. A two minute walk from Staples down Shaw Street will lead to the venue (on left opposite The Collegiate). The 21 and 345 from Queen Square travel along Shaw Street and will drop you off directly in front of the venue.

Rail:

The Creative Campus is around ten minutes walk from Liverpool's largest and main railway station, Liverpool Lime Street (and around seven minutes walk from the Norton Street National Express bus station). The main entrance to the Liverpool Lime Street is opposite Queen Square Bus Terminal from which you can travel by bus.

## Liverpool Everyman

Hope Street, Liverpool, Merseyside, L1 9BH

Tel: 0151 709 4776

The new Everyman is a reincarnation of the 400-seat theatre with its dynamic 'thrust' auditorium, including a rehearsal room, workshops, sound studio, Writers' Room, and a special studio dedicated to Young Everyman Playhouse, education and community groups. Above the iconic red sign, the exterior features

105 portraits of people from across Merseyside forming a unique piece of public art in an exceptionally green and accessible building.

With a history of providing Liverpool with radical ground-breaking theatre, the Everyman was founded in 1964 in an area of Liverpool noted for its bohemian environment and political edge. The astonishing range of talent to emerge from the Everyman includes Julie Walters, Bernard Hill, Jonathan Pryce, Pete Postlethwaite, Alison Steadman, Antony Sher, Bill Nighy, Alan Bleasdale, Willy Russell, Barbara Dickson, Matthew Kelly, Cathy Tyson, David Morrissey, Stephen Graham and the Liverpool Poets.

Its sister theatre is the Playhouse in Williamson Square and together they offer a programme of home grown work and the best in touring theatre

**Road Directions**
If you're driving, then use L1 9BH in your satnav to find the theatre, and ask the Box Office for details on where to park.

## Public Transport Directions
TRAVELLING BY BUS

The Citylink circular (CL) bus runs every 12 minutes during the daytime and into the early evening, every day, around Liverpool city centre and stops right outside The Everyman.

The following buses stop on Myrtle Street, just off Hope Street:

75, 80, 80A, 86, 86A, 86C, 139, 173

The following buses stop on Brownlow Hill, a 5 minute walk away:

6, 7, 7A, 14, 61, 79, 79C and 79D

If you're not on one of these routes, catch any bus into the city centre and jump on any of the above buses from various bus stops and bus stations in the city centre.

TRAVELLING BY TRAIN

Catch a Northern Line or Wirral Line train to Liverpool

Central station. From there, it's a 10 minute walk to The Everyman.

Catch a City Line or mainline train to Liverpool Lime Street station. From there, it's a 10 minute walk to The Everyman.

## Liverpool Empire Theatre

Lime Street, Liverpool, Merseyside, L1 1JE

Tel: 0844 871 3017

The Liverpool Empire Theatre is situated on Lime Street, the busy gateway road to Liverpool. It's ideally located within metres of Lime Street Station.

The Empire has the largest two-tier auditorium in Britain, seating 2348. It's the second theatre to be built on the site, with the previous smaller theatre demolished in 1924, today's building opened a year later in 1925. The orginal theatre was named 'The Prince of Wales Theatre and Opea House' and opened in 1866.

The theatre plays host to a number of big-name touring productions, musicals and concerts. Throughout the years the Empire has gone from strength to strength; showcasing the best in local, national and international talent.

## Liverpool Philharmonic Hall

Hope Street, Liverpool, Merseyside, L1 9BP

Tel: +44 (0)151 709 3789

The Liverpool Philharmonic Hall is an art-deco style Grade II listed building located on Liverpool's well-known and well-loved Hope Street within the city's Georgian Quarter.

In 1840, a group of Liverpool music lovers founded The Royal Liverpool Philharmonic. It is one of the world's oldest concert societies with the award-winning Royal Liverpool Philharmonic Orchestra at the heart of it along with its associated ensembles and concert series; the Royal Liverpool Philharmonic Choir; Liverpool Philharmonic Youth Company and Children's Choirs.

The Orchestra has a dynamic musical partnership with it's Russian Chief Conductor, Vasily Petrenko, hosting concerts in Liverpool, across the UK and all over the world.

But the 60 orchestral concerts a year is not all that takes place at 'the Phil', a wide range of classical, contemporary and roots music, rock, pop and folk music, an amazing unique cinema experience and a top stand-up comedy line-up also take to the stage.

In 2015, a refurbishment was completed, adding a new more intimate venue, Music Room. The Music Room hosts a wide range of concerts and events, complimenting the main Hall's programme. The space is designed to let audiences get closer to the music

## St George's Hall

St George's Place, Liverpool, Merseyside, L1 1JJ

Tel: +44 (0)151 225 6909

Delve into the very heart of Liverpool's UNESCO World Heritage St George's Quarter and you'll find one of the finest examples of neo-classical architecture in the world.

The Grade I listed St George's Hall, opposite Lime Street Station, stands 169ft long and 74ft wide with a tunnel vaulted ceiling the largest of its kind in the whole of Europe. Built in the early 1800s as a grand hub for music festivals and the Civil and Crown courts, St George's Hall has been at the very epicentre of Liverpool life ever since.

After a £23m refurbishment programme, this magnificent structure reopened its doors in 2007, returning to its former glory as an unrivalled spot for world-class events and happenings.

The interior architecture cannot be beaten; with a ceiling supported on massive red granite columns, and figures portraying qualities Victorian Liverpool aspired to - art, science, fortitude and justice. Look beyond the gold leaf and porticoes in the Great Hall; this is home to the greatest brick arches in the world, and houses a breath-taking Minton tiled floor of 30,000 mosaic tiles. Since the floor was uncovered back in 1954, the public has been able to glimpse it numerous times throughout years keep an eye out on our social channels for the next 'big reveal'!

Throughout the year, St George's Hall plays host to plenty of free and paid public events and exhibitions it's even a popular location for filming, so you might even stumble upon a set fit for Fantastic Beasts and Where to Find Them!

To really understand the workings and behind-the-scene wonders, we highly suggest booking yourself onto one of their tours. Explore the nooks and crannies of St George's Hall that the public rarely get to see by following their enthusiastic and knowledgeable tour guides that will tell you fascinating stories and lead you around the catacombs, cells and rooms of this magnificent building. Tours can be booked at the Heritage Centre and are easily tailored to meet requirements.

Planning on making it a whole day experience? Perfect! The café offers salads, freshly made sandwiches, cakes and pastries to keep you going, and you can pick up all of the Liverpool gifts you might need at The Heritage Centre.

Key features of the Heritage Centre include:

The original south entrance hall on St Johns Lane, designed by Harvey Lonsdale Elmes, but never before used by the public;

Opportunities to visit the cells used by prisoners awaiting trial;

The newly refurbished Criminal Court and Judge's Robing Room;

Glimpses of the unique ventilation system designed by Dr David Boswell Reid;

A new accessible viewing gallery for the Great Hall;

St George's Hall Café (open 7 days a week 8.30am 4.00pm)

## Liverpool Playhouse

Williamson Square, Liverpool, Merseyside, L1 1EL

Tel: +44 (0)151 709 4776

Built in 1866 as the Star Music Hall, in 1911 the Liverpool Playhouse housed one the first and later one of the longest running repertory companies in the country when it ended in 1999. The Playhouse's acting roster was among the finest in the country including Robert Donat, Michael Redgrave, Rachel Kempson, John Thaw, Anthony Hopkins and many, many more and the rich variety of the repertory programme formed many generations of committed theatregoers.

It was here that Noel Coward first worked with Gertrude Lawrence, as child actors, was the wartime home of the Old Vic company, and in the latter part of the twentieth century featured the tenure of 'The Gang of Four' Alan Bleasdale, Chris Bond, Bill Morrison and Willy Russell a brief but dazzlingly creative period which spawned, among many others, Russell's international smash hit, Blood Brothers.

In 1999, Liverpool's Everyman and Playhouse theatres were joined together in a new management created to take the city's producing theatre forward into the 21st century. Since 2004, the theatres have been on a remarkable journey, described as "a theatrical renaissance on Merseyside" (The Observer) with over 20 world premières, the majority by Liverpool writers.

## ROAD DIRECTIONS

Travelling by Car

If you're travelling from outside the city, follow signage for Queen Square or St John's Car Parks to reach the Playhouse

Car Parking

Playhouse patrons are entitled to a reduction at St Johns Car Parks: £2 after 5pm when you show your theatre ticket.

## Public Transport Directions

Travelling by Bus

The Playhouse is a few minutes walk from the bus stops at Queen Square and Sir Thomas Street. The new interchange for Paradise Street is now open and serves buses from across Merseyside.

Travelling by Train

Central Station which serves the Merseyrail network is a 5 minute walk to the Playhouse. Lime Street Station (Liverpool's main rail station) is also a 5 minute walk to the Playhouse.

## Royal Court Liverpool

1 Roe Street, Liverpool, Merseyside, L1 1HL

Tel: 0870 787 1866. Fax: 0870 787 1241

The Royal Court provides a unique theatre experience for any visitor to Liverpool. Dining in your seat before the show, drinks at your table and some of the very best Liverpool talent performing in home produced plays.

The Court produces eight shows a year with each one lasting four to six weeks. Generally comedies and musicals, this is the place to go for high quality entertainment using the best professional actors in the city. Actors rehearse in the city, sets are built here and 95% of money generated by the theatre is paid back into the city to staff and suppliers.

In 2012 the Royal Court Liverpool Trust invested £1.2m on the auditorium, replacing every seat and renovating the stalls bar area. In 2015 a further £2.8m was spent on front of house areas, replacing circle toilets and bars, a new Box Office, daytime cafe, foyer extension and a lift to all floors. More money is set to be invested in future to maintain this stunning Art Deco venue.

This venue is a must see for any visitor to the city, a look at real Liverpool theatre and a guaranteed great night of entertainment.

## Unity Theatre

1 Hope Place, Liverpool, Merseyside, L1 9BG

Tel: 0151 709 4988

unity is the most accessible venue in the city and has been in it's current home, the former synagogue in Hope Place, for 30 years.

Unity is a receiving house for professional and local theatre companies and provides a platform for small theatre companies. it boasts an excellent track record in encouraging new writing and supporting new companies.

unity holds a unique place in the cultural make up of the city, providing an eclectic mix of drama, dance, comedy, family friendly entertainment music and art.

Enhancing the quality of the performing arts on Merseyside by encouraging creativity, participation, innovation and diversity is written into unity's mission statement, and it has been described as 'The most ambitious theatre in Liverpool.' - The Guardian.

unity patrons include Sir Bill Kenwright CBE, David Morrissey, Andrew Lancel and Josette Bushell-Mingo.

## Road Directions

From the end of the M62 motorway follow the signs for the city centre and cathedrals, approx 3 miles. Turn left at the Metropolitan Cathedral and head past the Everyman Theatre and Philharmonic Hall, both on the left hand side along Hope Street. Hope Place is the first right turn off Hope Street after the Philharmonic Hall.

The nearest car park is ECP on Caledonia Street. There is also a car park on Hope Street/Myrtle Street plus on-street pay and display parking around Hope Place. Please note that Hope Place is residents only parking between 8am & 6pm.

## Public Transport Directions

Central Station and Lime Street train stations are a 15 minute walk away.

For timetable information call 0871 200 22 33. Arriva Buses 1 and 4 link Hope Street with Liverpool City Centre and both stations.

Other buses that stop nearby are:

74, 75, 80/80A, 82, 82A, B & E and 86/86A, B & C. For

public transport information go to merseytravel.gov.uk or call Merseylink on 0151 709 1929

# Music

This is a city that moves to its own rhythm; a city that's very heart beats with the sound of music. We're a UNESCO City of Music, famous for its Mersey Beat and for those four lads that changed the music world forever - but that's not all.

No Beatles fan can leave Liverpool unturned, and a pilgrimage to the city where it all began for those four boys is non-negotiable. A trip to The Beatles Story at the Albert Dock will journey you through The Beatles lives with its fascinating memorabilia, starting from their humble beginnings to the present day.

Ever fancied discovering the story of British music? Through costumes, instruments, performance and memorabilia, the British Music Experience at Liverpool's Pier Head brings the last 50 years of music right before your eyes. From Freddie Mercury to Dusty

Springfield, Adele and even the Spice Girls, Britain's musical prowess never looked so colourful.

You can't come to Liverpool and not visit the legendary cellar that has seen seven incredible decades of music (including The Beatles first performance on 9th February 1961). The Cavern Club is still the beating heart of Liverpool Beatle-Mecca of Mathew Street, while a combined tour of Lennon and McCartney's childhood homes - Mendips and 20 Forthlin Road - will allow you to explore where the boys met, composed and rehearsed many of their earliest songs.

The Liverpool music scene also includes the world-class M&S Bank Arena on the waterfront, which has attracted massive names like Bob Dylan, Beyonce and Paul McCartney. in the past.

And who could come to Liverpool and overlook the many festivals we host every year (many even being free). Liverpool International Music Festival (LIMF), Africa Oye, Sound City and International Beatleweek are just four of our favourites, but we'll let you discover the rest.

Have we mentioned we're also home to one of the finest orchestras in the country? The Royal Liverpool Philharmonic Orchestra, whose home is at the beautiful art deco Philharmonic Hall, frequently play in the city, while artists like Michael Kiwanuka, Squeeze and Goldie also frequent the Hall.

But don't get us wrong - it's not all about the big venues here. Many smaller venues throughout Liverpool host live music nights and open mic nights (we recommend checking out Arts Club, Buyers Club and The Magnet). Wherever you go, you're never too far away from music in this city.

## British Music Experience

Cunard Building, The Strand, Pier Head, Liverpool, Merseyside, L3 1QB

Tel: +44 (0)151 519 0915

The British Music Experience tells the story of British Music through costumes, instruments, performance and memorabilia. Whatever age you are, and whatever you are into, there is something here for you.

See outfits worn by artists from Freddie Mercury and Dusty Springfield, to the Spice Girls, Adam Ant and X Factor finalists and musical instruments played by some of the world's most renowned artists from Noel Gallagher to the Sex Pistols. There's even hand written song lyrics from Adele, the original statues from the Brits and the Apple Corp front door from Saville Row.

You can also get involved. You can learn a musical instrument with the best music equipment available, from drum kits to keyboards. Teenagers will love to try their hand at being a rock star by testing the vocal booth and smaller children can enjoy the show and dance the decades in our dance pop routines studio!

After the main event browse an exclusive range of gifts, clothing, books and memorabilia from the Merch

Store and you can rest those dancing feet with a selection of delicious snacks and meals in the Star Café.

Road Directions

Follow signs to Liverpool city centre, Albert Dock, Mersey Ferries. Several parking options around Albert Dock and Liverpool One. The Cunard Building is situated next to The Liver Building on the Waterfront. Entrance at the front of the building (river/Pierhead side).

Public Transport Directions

James Street station on Liverpool's underground link from Lime Street Station is just over the road from us.

## Cavern Club

10 Mathew Street, Liverpool, Merseyside, L2 6RE

Tel: 0151 236 1965

The legendary cellar that has seen seven incredible decades of music; from The Beatles first performance on 9th February 1961 to the Arctic Monkeys pre-breakthrough gig in October 2005, the Cavern Club remains the beating heart of Liverpool's iconic music scene.

The iconic stage beneath the brick arches in the front of the club is the image most people associate with the Cavern Club - and this is where you can enjoy live music from soloists and cover bands from mid-afternoon until late evening. Open 7 days a week from 10am, you'll experience everything from Rock n Roll to solo acoustic, as well as Cavern Club resident artists and top-class Merseybeat tribute acts. This is the place you need to be to truly experience the evocative spirit of the most famous club in the world.

From the Cavern Club, follow signs towards the Cavern Live Lounge where a state-of-the-art sound system is waiting to blare out the very best artists. Expect established acts, The Cavern Club Beatles tribute shows and plenty of legendary rock artists.

The third venue comes in the form of the Cavern Pub; open daily from 11am with a staggering amount of

Cavern and rock memorabilia on display, including live music every night that won't cost you a penny. Serving paninis, toasties, sandwiches, wraps and even quality hand raised pork pie, you've got no excuses to leave. Those of you who have had the pleasure of taking a trip aboard the Magical Mystery Tour can also receive 10% off your food bill by simply show your boarding card to a member of staff upon ordering too.

Last but by no means least is the all important souvenir shop. No trip to the Cavern can be without it, and you can take with you merchandise including t-shirts, CDs, books, pin badges and postcards.

For that special occasion whether it be birthdays, anniversaries or for business the venue is available for private hire.

Take a virtual tour around the Cavern Club with 'The Cavern Club Chronicles' from Expedia, and explore all that's on offer!

## The Beatles Story

Britannia Vaults, Royal Albert Dock, Liverpool,

Merseyside, L3 4AD

Tel: +44 (0)151 709 1963

The award-winning 'The Beatles Story' is the world's largest permanent exhibition purely devoted to telling the story of The Beatles' rise to fame. Located in the Fab Four's hometown of Liverpool on the stunning UNESCO World heritage waterfront at the Albert Dock, The Beatles Story takes visitors on an immersive journey through the lives, times, culture and music of the world's greatest band.

Join The Beatles on their journey; first conquering Liverpool, and then the world, through recreations of key locations from the band's career including The Casbah Club, The Cavern Club, and Abbey Road Studios.

Multi-media audio guides are available in eleven different languages including English, French, German,

Italian, Japanese, Mandarin, Polish, Russian, Spanish, Brazilian Portuguese and more recently, Korean.

They are beautifully narrated by John Lennon's sister, Julia. The FREE guide is packed with information, imagery, and features video interviews with Paul McCartney and Ringo Starr, giving visitors a unique insight into the story of the Fab Four.

A must for any music fan, The Beatles Story features an impressive collection of fascinating memorabilia including the band's original instruments, John Lennon's New York piano, Ringo Starr's drum kit, rare album sleeves, photography and original lyrics.

New items recently introduced include the original Strawberry Field Gates, the 'Holy Grail' record that launched The Beatles, Brian Epstein's Jacket and to mark 50 years since the release of Sgt Pepper, a range of new memorabilia including a full set of authentic replica suits.

Finish your perfect historical experience in one of two Beatles-themed Fab4 Cafes or browse through a fantastic range of products available from one of the Fab4 Stores.

In 2018, The Beatles Story celebrates 50 years since The Beatles travelled to India with the launch of a special exhibition. 'Beatles In India' looks at this key period in time with new memorabilia, imagery and personal accounts from people who were there with them.

# Climate

The coastal town is located around 200 miles north of London, but experiences a much more temperate climate than continental Europe at the same latitude. Scandinavian countries experience more dramatic temperature changes from season to season, as well as longer lasting heat waves and cold snaps. Built on sandstone hills, Liverpool rises 230 feet above sea level at its highest point. Several estuaries border Liverpool that flow out into Liverpool Bay and the Irish Sea.

All the seasons here are generally mild, with cool summers and gentle winters. The tradeoff for temperate climate is daily weather that is highly unpredictable. No matter what time of year you are traveling, there's an equal chance of rain, sun, wind gusts or cloudy days. For the most part, temperatures hover around 60 degrees (15.5ºC) in the summertime and 40 degrees (4.5ºC) in the winter. It's rare for the daily temperature to rise above 74 degrees (23.3ºC) or fall below 27 degrees (-2.75ºC).

The tourist season tends to be in late spring and summer. This is the best chance at good weather, but early autumn can be less crowded and still have enjoyable weather. Mild humidity makes precipitation likely, so it's a good idea to check daily forecasts and carry protection against the rain. Travelers may do better to have some flexibility in their daily plans, saving museums and indoor landmarks in case of rainstorms and poor weather.

May, June and July have the best chances for sunny days, but there's still an average of 16 days of precipitation a month. During those 16 days, approximately two to five inches of precipitation fall.

# Travel to Liverpool

## To Get in

By plane

Liverpool John Lennon Airport has around 160 flights arriving daily from within the UK and Europe. The airport is well-served by low-cost airlines, particularly Easyjet and Ryanair.

There are regular bus services (80A,86A and the 500) from the airport to Liverpool South Parkway Rail Station (stand 4) A single costs £2.50. From the station there are regular services to Liverpool Lime Street and Manchester Stations.

Manchester Airportis about a 45-60 minute drive away from Liverpool. Hourly, direct rail services operate between Liverpool Lime Street Station and Manchester Airport operated by Northern Rail. Manchester Airport has a wide variety of destinations. Frequent flights operate to North America and Asia, as well as short haul services throughout Europe.

As always,don't change money into £ Sterling at airports unless unavoidable-ripoff rates guaranteed at airport bureaux de change.There are ATMS (Cashpoints in British English) at both Liverpool and Manchester airports.Anywhere in the UK,do not accept £50 notes (impossible to use at shops or businesses,just maybe in hotels),always ask for notes of £20 or less.If arriving from the Eurozone,€ 200 or €500 notes will probably be impossible to change,even at banks or bureaux de change, anywhere in the UK.

By boat

Cruise liner ships berth in Liverpool City Centre, near the Pier Head. A new cruise liner facility has been constructed to enable bigger vessels to visit, and to enhance the experience.

Regular, scheduled ferries operate all year round, to and from

Douglas, in the Isle of Man operated by the SteamPacket Company. These depart from Douglas to Liverpool at 15:00, arriving 17:45. The return journey from Liverpool to Douglas is at 19:15, arriving 22:00. Foot passenger single fares range from £39.00 to £48.00. At quieter times of the year, special promotional "footloose" fares can usually be found for around £20.00.

Belfast, (Northern Ireland) operated by Stena Line. Foot passenger single fares range from £30.00 at quiet times of the year, to £45.00 throughout July and August and at other busier periods. Motor vehicles are also conveyed. Journey duration for the following services is 8 hours: Depart from Belfast to Liverpool and Liverpool to Belfast at *10:30 and 22:30.* Note: the

10:30 sailings do not operate on Monday(s) in either direction.

If arriving from Belfast,most businesses in Liverpool (especially taxi drivers) will not accept Northern Ireland banknotes

Dublin, (Republic of Ireland) operated by Sea Truck Ferries, crossing time takes 8 hours.

By train

Liverpool is well served by frequent rail services to/from Birmingham (1h40), Leeds (1h40), London (2h10), Manchester (45mins), Newcastle (3h), Nottingham (2h30), and York, (2h30). If travelling from Scotland, you'll change at either Wigan, Warrington or Preston See [www.nationalrail.co.uk National Rail] for details.

The principal station in Liverpool is 'Liverpool Lime Street'.

This is an impressive glass and steel building, a fine example of Victorian Engineering.

Facilities include - ticket office, travel information centre, help desks, left luggage, toilets, shops, cafes, pubs and coffee and fast food kiosks. There is a waiting room, 1st class lounge and cash machines between platforms 7 and 8.

There is a taxi rank at the Skelhorne St entrance to the station.

Pedestrian access is from Lime St, Lord Nelson St or Skelhorne St.

Trains depart for

London - 1 per hour Birmingham - 2 per hour Manchester - frequent Liverpool South Parkway (for John Lennon Airport) - frequent Leeds - 2 per hour Wigan - 3 per hour

Lime Street also has an underground station on the conurbation's Merseyrail network, where Wirral Line trains depart for Chester, Ellesmere Port, West Kirby, and New Brighton. If you need Northern Line trains to Southport, Ormskirk, Kirkby and Hunts Cross (via

Liverpool South Parkway for John Lennon Airport), take the Wirral Line one stop to Liverpool Central and change there.

By coach

National Express, the UK's largest scheduled coach company operates services from the city's Liverpool ONE bus station. London is four to five hours away by coach and is served by a half a dozen services per day. Manchester is served by an hourly service taking a similar time to the train (except at rush hour). Manchester Airport can be reached by coach in under one hour, six coaches run per day.

Megabus operates a network across the U.K. There is one bus daily from London to Liverpool. Journey time 4-5 hours. Prices also start at £1 and then increase depending on how far in advance you book.

By bus

Micro bus to Poland. Alternative connection by land from to Warsaw, and other major cities in Central and Eastern Europe. Price £70.

## To Get around

Airport Bus Links

Liverpool John Lennon Airport has regular bus links into Liverpool City Centre, provided by Arriva. It is recommended that you board the dedicated "Airlink" express service, "500", primarily because it only takes around 30 minutes into the City Centre, with no intermediate stops and it is fairly frequent. The 500 express bus will cost around £3-4 single, payable in cash. Unfortunately the express service does not operate after around 19:00.

Other (Arriva) bus services operate into Liverpool City Centre, (80A and 86A), but these are local stopping services, taking around 50-60 minutes to reach the City Centre. They are slightly cheaper, costing around £2-3 for a single. These buses run from around 05:00 until midnight.

Other local bus services operate towards Bootle, (81A), Walton, (81A), Huyton, (89A), and St. Helens, (89A). A coach service operates towards Manchester.

It is possible to buy a one day travel ticket for buses and trains at the airport information desk for £3.70 this is valid on all buses including the 500 airport express. Ask for a zone C saveaway. If you want to use the ferry ask for an all zone saveaway for £4.70. This is actually cheaper than a single ferry fare.

Taxis from JLA have a £1 surcharge levied by the airport,so whatever your fare,it will be that + £1.Standard fares are on a sign in the terminal.If there are 3-4 of you,get a cab rather than the bus.

Taxis
Liverpool City Centre is not too big to walk around, but black hackney cabs are plentiful if you are feeling lazy. You can usually hail a hackney cab from the side of the

road, but in busier areas, these taxis will have a designated pick up area.

Private hire taxis are also available, but must be booked by telephone, although some of the bigger companies now have their own app for booking taxis. They are often significantly cheaper than a black hackney cab. It usually takes no longer than 5-10 minutes for a private hire taxi to arrive, after you have booked it by telephone.

Like elsewhere in the UK, Both hackney and private hire taxis are strictly regulated. Hackney cabs should always use the meter, (unless you are travelling a particularly long distance), and most private hire taxis will have a table showing the price(s) per mile and any other charges. It is unlikely you will be intentionally overcharged. Hand written receipts are usually available.

Local Bus Services

Many bus services operate in and around Liverpool. The most popular (and frequent) routes are primarily operated by *Stagecoach Merseyside* or *Arriva North West* using modern, low floor vehicles. Cash single fares are usually under £3.00, unless you are travelling outside of Liverpool. Student tickets available for £1.80 for Arriva services and £1.70 for Stagecoach services. If you don't plan to get around by bus and you are a student then it is the cheapest option. You should pay the driver as you board. You should avoid paying for bus fares with banknotes. £20 notes are not usually accepted and £50 notes will never be accepted. Try to pay using coins. If you are unsure of when to get off, speak to the bus driver when boarding, and ask if he can tell you when you arrive. Most bus drivers will be happy to do this. Liverpool day pass for Arriva buses £4.20,weekly pass £17 (Aug 2017). Stagecoach weekly pass cost £14.50

Most local bus numbers ending in "A", e.g. 80A, 82A, 86A, 89A etc. will eventually call at, (or terminate at), the Airport. Routes ending in "B", "C", "D" usually indicate the bus takes a slightly different route, for example, the 82 bus does not serve Queen Square bus station, but the 82D service does. Routes ending in "E" usually do not run the full length of the route.

Bus numbers starting with "N", (e.g. N5, N37), are Night Buses, provided by Arriva. They operate only on Friday and Saturday nights until around 4am and all depart from Queen Square Bus station. Night Bus fares are relatively expensive, £4-£5 for a cash single. No other tickets are accepted.

There are two main bus stations in the City Centre, these are operated by Merseytravel. Both have a travel information centre, stocked with timetables and tourist information leaflets. You can also purchase daily, weekly, monthly and annual public transport tickets, as well as National Express coach tickets.

Liverpool ONE Bus Station, located in the Liverpool ONE shopping complex, has very frequent bus services operating towards the suburbs in South Liverpool, (e.g. Runcorn/Speke/Garston/Halewood/Liverpool Airport).

The 500 Airport Express service calls here.

Queen Square Bus Station is situated near Liverpool Lime Street station and St. John's Shopping Centre. It is a short walk away from the Liverpool ONE shopping area. Most services departing from here are operating towards North Liverpool,

(e.g. Walton/Fazakerley/Croxteth/Kirkby/Huyton).

You can also board the Liverpool Airport Express service from here.

Rail Services

Good, frequent rail services operate from Liverpool City Centre. "Peak time" in Liverpool is between 06:30 and 09:30, and between 16:30 and 18:00. During these times, some local rail tickets may become more expensive and services will be busy.

Liverpool Central is the busiest underground station on the conurbation's Merseyrail Network, and gives access to both Northern and Wirral Lines. Trains on Merseyrail Wirral and Northern Lines run every 15 minutes to each end destination, forming higher frequencies as the services converge closer to the centre of the conurbation. Fares are typical for "local journeys" (around the £2 to £5 cost typically). For all day travel across all buses, trains and ferries in the city area, ask for a "Saveaway" ticket from any train station or Merseytravel centre in the city area. This costs just over £5.

Liverpool Lime Street is the terminus for most long distance services from places like Birmingham, London, Nottingham, Manchester, Leeds and York. Local trains also depart from Lime Street, heading towards Huyton, St Helens, Warrington and Wigan. Some routes can be infrequent, but most long distance destinations have at least an hourly service, with the local routes usually around every 15 minutes. Lime Street also has an underground station served by all branches of the Merseyrail Wirral Line.

The End